MIRACLES IN THE CHRISTIAN TRADITION

Owen F. Cummings

Paulist Press
New York / Mahwah, NJ

Cover design by Joe Gallagher
Book design by Lynn Else

Library of Congress Cataloging-in-Publication Data
Names: Cummings, Owen F., author.
Title: Miracles in the Christian tradition / Owen F. Cummings.
Description: New York / Mahwah, NJ : Paulist Press, 2021. | Summary: "Hoping to overcome what John Meier refers to as the 'academic sneer factor' when speaking of the miraculous, Owen Cummings examines the history of the miraculous from the Old Testament through attitudes of twenty-first century theologians"— Provided by publisher.
Identifiers: LCCN 2020018817 (print) | LCCN 2020018818 (ebook) | ISBN 9780809155309 (paperback) | ISBN 9781587689260 (ebook)
Subjects: LCSH: Miracles—History of doctrines. | Miracles—Biblical teaching.
Classification: LCC BT97.3 .C96 2021 (print) | LCC BT97.3 (ebook) | DDC 231.7/3—dc23
LC record available at https://lccn.loc.gov/2020018817
LC ebook record available at https://lccn.loc.gov/2020018818

ISBN 978-0-8091-5530-9 (paperback)
ISBN 978-1-58768-926-0 (e-book)

Published by Paulist Press
997 Macarthur Boulevard
Mahwah, New Jersey 07430
www.paulistpress.com

Printed and bound in the
United States of America

Dedicated to the miracles in my life:
Cathy, *sine qua non*
Andrew
Anne
Owen
Susan
Mary

CONTENTS

CHAPTER 1

MIRACLES

An Introduction

> If there is an irreducible core of the miraculous in Christian belief, then that belief must inevitably face up to the philosophical and other problems which cluster around the concept.
>
> Ninian Smart[1]

> To assert that miracles cannot happen is no more rational—and no less an act of faith—than to assert that they can and do happen.
>
> Kenneth Woodward[2]

We find accounts of miracles throughout the entirety of the Christian tradition, beginning with the Bible, both Testaments. A minimal understanding of miracle is that it is "an extraordinary event," an event that does not count as ordinary or usual in the daily round of happenings. Further qualification of that minimal definition is required, especially theological qualification, but it will do for the moment. We can also find accounts of miracles in many other religious traditions, but this book is concerned only with the Christian tradition.[3] It is concerned not only with just the Christian tradition but also, in view of the massive range of publications on the topic, with a very selective reading of that tradition, snapshots of that tradition if you will.

DID MIRACLES HAPPEN? DO MIRACLES HAPPEN?

Did miracles happen? Do miracles happen? Two very fair questions, but questions that do not easily admit of immediate black-and-white answers for a reflective modern person. "A wise man proportions his belief to the evidence."[4] This simple and straightforward commonsense comment from Scottish philosopher of religion Ninian Smart (1927–2001), echoing David Hume, helps us to get the ball rolling when it comes to thinking about miracles. Briefly, Smart is telling us or, better, reminding us what every person knows—we think things through, at least sometimes. We do not simply accept explanations of events that do not make sense to us in terms of our immediate experience and understanding. No, we sift explanations and hypotheses. We try to find a way of understanding phenomena that is both satisfying and persuasive from an intellectual point of view, but an intellectual point of view within the horizon of Christian faith. That is what we are trying to do in this book.

Christian faith, at least as traditionally understood, has always accepted the miraculous, especially because of the miraculous element in the Gospels. What I am attempting in this book is an understanding of these traditions of the miraculous that are both true to Christian faith and true to our contemporary experience and understanding of reality. It cannot be one at the expense of the other if you are a Christian. If we are simply intent on handing on the truths of the Christian faith as we have received them without any intellectual sifting whatsoever, that is fideism, accepting things simply on the say-so of someone else, however important and magisterial that someone else happens to be. If, on the other hand, we screen out truths of the faith on the basis of our own personal or individual concept of rationality in an a priori fashion, that is tantamount to rational solipsism, the understanding that we, basically on our own, have completely understood all there is to be understood. Both fideism and rational solipsism are to be avoided.

It is simply a statement of fact that miracles have been reported, discussed, and critiqued over the two-thousand-year duration of the Christian tradition. Critique is certainly not a new phenomenon, though undoubtedly negative critique is far more common nowadays. At the same time, the absolute certitude that miracles cannot happen and do not happen and, therefore, did not happen is certainly going beyond what may be regarded as the normal boundaries of human knowledge. Laying out what may be the boundaries of human knowledge is not as simple or straightforward as it might seem. Yes, there is a straightforward knowledge about whether X is an apple or an orange, or whether the spaghetti I ordered from the menu is in fact spaghetti or not. There is no dispute about such knowledge, about straightforward matters of fact. But when one moves beyond these rather pedestrian observations, the boundaries of human knowledge shift. Think, for example, of history. "Historical statements can reach a very high degree of probability. They never attain logical certainty in the sense that they cannot be denied without a logical contradiction. It is not logically possible to deny that a circle is circular, but it is always possible to deny that an alleged historical event took place."[5] Furthermore, seriously differing interpretations of historical events are given. Think, for example, of the Crusades in the Middle Ages. Those invasions of the Holy Land look different when viewed through a Muslim lens over against a traditional Christian/Western historiographical lens. The communities of historical scholars exist in order to regulate and finally to judge appropriately concerning historical events. With respect to the biblical miracles, the communities of biblical scholars exist in order to regulate and finally to judge appropriately the historicity of the accounts, and we shall have occasion to look at some of their contributions. Knowledge of history is not the same as knowledge of mathematics. Things get weighed differently. The patristic scholar Joseph T. Lienhard, SJ, makes the point well about knowing and loving other persons: "There are some sorts of knowledge that can only follow commitment, love, and risk. The absurdity of a young man saying to a young woman, 'I would like, first, to know everything about you that can be known, and then I shall decide whether or not I love you,' is patent." Lienhard goes on to make a similar point about the Bible, in which we find the miracle stories of Jesus. He writes, "The same is true of the Bible. Thus, the first problem with the historical method: of itself, it can only affirm discrete facts from the past. As such, it cannot provide the foundation for faith. Two choices remain: either to abandon faith, or to fall into fideism."[6] We do not wish to abandon Christian faith, and we do not wish to fall into fideism. Trying to steer a path between these two positions is far from easy, but it is what we are attempting to do in this book.

In the introduction to his extremely well argued book *Reported Miracles*, Scottish philosophical theologian Joseph Houston writes as follows: "Although he will have specialist expertise in one or two areas, a systematic theologian cannot engage in detailed careful scrutiny of all the current views of all the specialists whom he must consult: biblical scholars, historians of doctrine and the philosophy, experts in other religions than his own, and philosophers."[7] The point is well made and well taken. It is impossible for the systematic theologian to be in command and control of all pertinent writing on almost any subject in the field, and this is certainly true of miracles. So much has happened in the disciplines mentioned by Houston in the last century or so that one must be extremely selective in the issues, areas, and scholars to which and to whom one attends. With this caveat in mind, let us now move on by attempting a more nuanced definition of *miracle* than the one offered a moment ago, "an extraordinary event."

TOWARD A MORE NUANCED DEFINITION

Because of differing presuppositions that enter into an understanding of what a miracle is, it is exceedingly hazardous to offer a definition that would be agreeable to all parties who might be interested in commenting on the miraculous. However, the prolific and preeminent New Testament scholar John P. Meier provides us with a good starting point, a starting point in one of the most comprehensive and even-handed accounts of miracle in any work by any contemporary New Testament scholar. According to Meier's working definition a *miracle* is

1. an unusual, startling, or an extraordinary event that is in principle perceivable by any interested and fair-minded observer;
2. an event that finds no reasonable explanation in human abilities or in other known forces that operate in our world of time and space; and

> 3. an event that is the result of a special act of God, doing what no human power can do.[8]

Meier's is a broad definition indeed, and it covers all aspects of the issue that seem relevant. Number 3 brings his definition fairly and squarely into the realm of systematic theology. This last issue, the question of whether something is a result of a special act of God inexplicable in any other terms is of central interest to the theologian. Perhaps this is the point to acknowledge a caveat regarding "special acts of God inexplicable in any other terms" at the level of what we might describe as "popular religiosity." People are often attracted to what may seem to be "supernatural" happenings, for example, apparitions, healings, visions, and so forth. Such special acts are often approached with a degree of skepticism on the part not only of theologians but also of church authorities. As Louis Monden has acknowledged, "Even within the Catholic Church, excesses in popular devotional life have shown themselves in such guise as to require that warnings be issued from very high quarters in order that this fevered search for the marvelous be discountenanced."[9] Institutions are no less incredulous than individuals.

Who is to say for certain what may or may not happen, or what has or has not happened? John Meier very carefully states a distinction that he makes between the judgment of a historian, even a believing or Christian historian, and the judgment of a theologian.

> I maintain that…it is inherently impossible for historians working with empirical evidence within the confines of their own discipline ever to make the positive judgment: "God has directly acted here to accomplish something beyond all human power." The very wording of this statement shows that it is

> essentially *theo*-logical....What evidence and criteria could justify a historian *as a historian* in reaching such a judgment? To be sure, a professional historian who is likewise a believing Christian might proceed from one judgment ("this extraordinary event, occurring in a religious context, has no discernible explanation") to a second judgment ("this event is a miracle worked by God"). But this further judgment is not made in his or her capacity as a professional historian. The judgment that this particular event is a miracle accomplished by God necessarily moves the person making the judgment into the realm of philosophy or theology.[10]

This is very fair indeed. The historian may judge in view of all the sources available that such and such an event is accurately reported in the sources. The historian cannot move, however, from the judgment of historical accuracy or verisimilitude to the explanatory judgment that the event in question is a divine action.

However, having acknowledged that, the central question is this: "What constitutes an act of God so that it may be called a miracle?" or, as expressed by a contemporary Christian philosopher of religion, "In its bluntest form, the question that faces contemporary believers, or would-be believers, is whether they are prepared to countenance the idea of supernatural intervention."[11] These are the words of the philosopher John Cottingham, and for many people they express the crux of the problem of miracles, that is, the idea that God acts at particular points in time and in particular events to bring about his purposes. While Cottingham goes on to say that Christians need not go to the stake for every miraculous event recounted in the Bible, there do appear to be some such events that are absolutely central to what is normally understood as orthodox Christian faith, and he is thinking especially of the resurrection of Jesus.

Another perspective on the miraculous emerges from people's ordinary lived experience. A natural and positive response from Christian people is to turn to God, especially when life's circumstances become very difficult and problematic, and ask for divine help. This is encouraged by Jesus in the Gospels: "Ask, and it will be given you" (Matt 7:7). Sometimes when Christians are going through the experience of dealing with terminal illness, for example, they pray for a miracle. They ask God—or, in the case of Catholics, their request to God may be made through the intercession of the Blessed Virgin Mary or some other saint—to effect a cure. This is a very understandable emotional reaction on the part of a Christian believer in the face of impending death. At the same time, it must be acknowledged that those who pray for a miraculous cure are also often quite resigned to the prospect that it will not happen. They may add to their prayerful request, "if it is the will of God." At the very least, though it is often much more, this is an acknowledgment of both our lack of self-sufficiency in life and our fragility and vulnerability. It is an awareness of our dependence on that which is other than ourselves, an awareness of God, who cares about his creatures. This is a good thing. Nonetheless, serious questions may be raised. Where is God in all of this? That really is the central question. How is God at work in creation, and, more particularly, how is God at work in what are regarded as miraculous events? Responses to some of these questions will unfold in the subsequent chapters of this book.

CHAPTER 2

MIRACLES IN THE OLD TESTAMENT

Where the analysis of the event depends upon its exact reconstruction, it is usually impossible to determine "exactly what happened."...Critical and historical elements are therefore of primary importance and impose caution in the study of the miraculous in Hebrew tradition.

John L. McKenzie[1]

There is a danger that in using the familiar English word "miracle" with reference to the Hebrew Bible one may import familiar implications and overtones from historic debates—such as Hume's famous definition of a miracle as "a violation of the laws of nature," although the notion of an autonomous natural world was unknown to the writers of the Hebrew Bible.

Walter L. Moberly[2]

INTRODUCTION

These opening remarks of two different generations of highly respected biblical scholars, John McKenzie (1910–91) and Walter Moberly (born in 1952, and professor of Old Testament in the University of Durham, UK), set the tone for this chapter. From McKenzie we learn that while it is natural since at least the time of the Enlightenment to inquire of our biblical sources to find out exactly what happened, absolute certitude is impossible. The skills of historical criticism come into play and always result in degrees of probability, not historical exactitude. From Moberly we are warned not to import into the writings of the Old Testament the concerns of later ages. With Moberly we must "proceed with caution,"[3] recognizing that the so-called natural world was permeated by the presence and activity of God for the Hebrews. The natural world was never just "natural" in the sense of reality utterly distinct from and unrelated to the fundamental conviction of God as present and active. The fundamental perspective of the Old Testament Scriptures is that God is always faithful, always at work in both nature and history, even when the Israelites did not make that distinction hard and fast, and God's faithfulness always exceeds human faithfulness.[4] The distinguished New Testament scholar Luke Timothy Johnson writes, "In the stories, songs, and prophecies composed by God's faithful over the long history of Israel, we find not only many accounts of miracles, but above all the shaping of the imaginative world that enables the perception of *God as continuously active within his creation*."[5] In line with the perspective of Moberly, Johnson, and others, all of the Old Testament writings, albeit with varying degrees of intensity, manifest this continuous presence and activity of God in creation, in the election and history of Israel. Nowhere is God absent, and so anywhere/anything may become a manifest sign of his presence and action, his presence and power.

This point of view has implications for how we read the text of the Old Testament. Reading it from the perspective of modern historiography will often (and one might argue necessarily) be fueled by a hermeneutic of suspicion, even if, as Johnson argues, "there are good reasons for asserting at least the broad lines of the narrative as having some basis in the actual experience of the people (of Israel)."[6] Reading the Old Testament through the lens of a committed believer will yield, by way of contrast, what Johnson calls a "hermeneutics of generosity or charity." This is how he describes it:

> Throughout this book I am practicing what is sometimes called a hermeneutics of generosity or charity, which seeks to find in the texts, with all the difficulties they pose to our (shared) modern outlook, the wisdom that God's Holy Spirit expresses through them. Since my thesis from the start has been that God's presence and power *is* in truth being manifested in creation even today, my approach to these mythic narratives is not one of explaining away the miraculous, but of discerning the experiential origins and the religious understandings expressed by these accounts, so that they can help us in our world "imagine the world that Scripture imagines" and see our own experience and our own world in terms of that same presence and power.[7]

I am very sympathetic to this "hermeneutics of generosity or charity," but at the same time I think it is necessary to engage, in some fashion, those accounts of "miracle" in a narrower, post-Enlightenment perspective, to engage, if you like, something of a "hermeneutic of suspicion."

Miracles are infrequent occurrences in the Old Testament. There are the miracles associated with Moses and Joshua and those associated with Elijah and Elisha. One might add to them the marvelous events described in Isaiah 37:36–37 and 38:7–8. Even in these contexts, however, the miraculous signs are understood to give support to the messengers of God's word. It is God's word that is of supreme importance, and these extraordinary events are signs of the efficacy of that word. God's word works! The miraculous signs not only confirm God's word of faithfulness to Israel but also are to be understood as signs of his love for his people. Consider, for example, the following passages from the Psalms:

> Our ancestors, when they were in Egypt,
> did not consider your wonderful works;
> they did not remember the abundance of your steadfast love,
> but rebelled against the Most High at the Red Sea. (Ps 106:7)

and

> Let them thank the LORD for his steadfast love,
> for his wonderful works to humankind.
> (Ps 107:8)

The wonderful deeds performed by God for Israel are to be understood as the working out of his love for his people. The Psalms, composed and revised over some five hundred years, were (and are) used in worship, and these sentiments of the worshipers manifest their commitment to God and their confidence in God's commitment to them, both in the past and in the present. The presence and action of God throughout all the life of believers is truly "wonder-filled."

Consider these words of theologian Gerald O'Collins about the Psalms:

> They make visible in prayer the invisible drama of the self and the community when face-to-face with God. Going to the heart of who we are as human beings, they enjoyed the immediacy and power of personal testimony....These poetic prayers record a range of ways in which human beings received, responded to, and interpreted the divine revelation that came through history, creation, and wisdom thought....At the heart of the Psalms is the loving faithfulness of God that the Israelites experienced in events of history and works of creation. The psalmists felt guarded against despair by the powerful kindness of their God.[8]

That last sentence is especially compelling. O'Collins is talking specifically about the Psalmists, but what he is saying of them is equally applicable to the worshiping people of Israel as a whole—they experienced "the powerful kindness of their God." We wish to go somewhat further, however, and so let us now turn to the narrower sense of miracle in the accounts of Moses and Joshua.

MOSES AND JOSHUA

Read superficially, the Books of Exodus and Joshua, centering on the key characters of Moses and Joshua, seem to provide a fairly straightforward history of the movement of the people of Israel from slavery in Egypt across the Red Sea, through their meanderings in the desert, and finally to their crossing the river Jordan and entering into the land of

Canaan. If these narratives are treated primarily in historical terms using a hermeneutic of suspicion, the historian comes up against some serious challenges and problems. Immediately the historian must come to terms with the specific parallels that are drawn between Moses and Joshua.

- From the desert, Moses sent out spies to scout the land (Num 13; Deut 1:19–46); from Transjordan, Joshua sent out spies to scout out the territory near Jericho (Josh 2).
- With Moses as leader, the Israelites passed through the waters of the Red Sea as though they were on dry ground (Exod 14); with Joshua as leader, the Israelites crossed the river Jordan as though they were on dry ground (Josh 3).
- Just before the Exodus from Egypt, Moses and the Israelites celebrated the Passover (Exod 12); after they entered the land of Canaan, Joshua and the Israelites celebrated the Passover (Josh 5:10–12).
- The command to Moses, "Remove the sandals from your feet, for the place on which you are standing is holy ground" (Exod 3:5), finds its parallel verbatim when the commander of the army of the Lord said to Joshua, "Remove the sandals from your feet, for the place where you stand is holy" (Josh 5:15).

These parallels present Joshua "as little more than a kind of carbon copy of Moses" and certainly raise suspicions about historicity.[9] However, behind this carbon-copy understanding of Moses and Joshua remains the profound theological conviction that God is faithful and constant, is always with his people and their leaders, and is never absent. The primary understanding behind these parallels is God's constancy and faithfulness and presence.

These parallels are not the only ground for being critical of historical exactitude in the narratives. Other challenges present themselves. For example, one thinks of the Exodus of the Hebrew slaves from Egypt itself and then their miraculous crossing of the Red Sea. The problem for the historian is that there is no account of these events outside the biblical text itself. The Irish scholar John J. Collins, Holmes Professor of Old Testament Criticism and Interpretation at Yale Divinity School and author of a widely used introduction to the Old Testament/Hebrew Scriptures, writes, "While it might be argued that the escape of the Israelites was inconsequential for the Egyptians, and therefore not recorded, in fact the Egyptians kept tight control over their eastern border and kept careful records. If a large group of Israelites had departed, we should expect some mention of it."[10] There is no such account. Furthermore, the genre of the Exodus narratives is the stuff of legend and folklore. This leads John Collins to comment as follows: "The story is replete with miraculous incidents, from the rescue of Moses from the Nile, to the burning bush, to the contest with the magicians of Egypt, to the crossing of the sea. The story of the baby Moses found in the bulrushes is a common folkloric motif. A similar story was told of King Sargon of Akkad (ca. 2300 BCE), whose mother also placed him in a vessel of reeds in a river."[11] Finally, we need to be alert to the fact that the final edition of the Book of Exodus comes from the time of the Babylonian Exile, more than seven hundred years after the events narrated. The memories of these historical events, and surely there must be some nucleus of historicity since nothing comes from nothing, so to speak, has been treasured and cherished and recited in the liturgical life of ancient Israel, since the cult is the primary locus for recalling the particular moments of God's providential action. The miraculous aspects in the narratives associated with Moses and Joshua have as their purpose the praising of Israel's God for his action in the past and the encouragement of hope in this God for his accompanying of his people now and in the future. In other words, and again without denying some irretrievable historical nucleus behind them, these miraculous actions of God are to be understood primarily as doxological and theological, not historical.

Nonetheless, a few commentators have gone to considerable lengths to underscore the historical probability of these miracle stories from Exodus and Joshua, for example, the physicist Sir Colin Humphreys. In a book entitled *The Miracles of Exodus: A Scientist's Discovery of the Extraordinary Natural Causes of the Biblical Stories*, Humphreys writes, "A natural explanation of the events of the Exodus doesn't to my mind make them any less miraculous. As we will see, the ancient Israelites believed that their God worked in, with, and through natural events. What made certain natural events miraculous was their timing: for example, the river Jordan stopped flowing precisely when the Israelites were assembled on its banks and desperate to cross.…I believe this natural explanation (an earthquake's blocking the flow of the Jordan) makes this miracle more, not less, believable."[12] To respond adequately to Humphreys's point of view would take us too far off course and, furthermore, lead us into a nexus of complex hermeneutical and theological explanations from scholarly perspectives that love the scriptural text no less than Humphreys does but come at them from a more sophisticated—and I would argue much more persuasive—standpoint. Here I simply want to acknowledge that such literalist accounts of the biblical narratives continue to be held by modern people.

That standpoint is certainly not uniform in the scholarly community, and the consensus of scholarship would probably take the following lines. First, there are no interventions, miraculous actions, "acts of God" in the history of Israel in the sense of specific events not intelligible or explicable by a historian of the ancient Near East. Second, what one might call the "locus" of revelation in the history of Israel was the religious consciousness of the people of Israel, and not in specific and particular outside events discernible to the neutral eye, so to speak. The words of the late English Jesuit theologian John Coventry are particularly helpful here:

> There are no interventions or "acts of God" in the history of Israel, in the sense of events not explicable by the secular historian. But of course...the secular historian must operate within categories proper to secular history. The suggestion will be that there are further dimensions of meaning open to discovery in secular events. The "locus" of revelation in Israel's history was solely the religious consciousness of Israel: in their minds (in the broad sense of their human appreciation) and not in particular outside events. By this is meant, not that God existed solely in their minds, but that God's Spirit acted in or on their minds to discern him in events otherwise secular.[13]

If miraculous signs are understood to demonstrate God's love for his people, that love relationship is celebrated especially in cult or liturgy. That is an important point because liturgical narratives/texts do not aim at precise and accurate historiography. Liturgical texts have to do with the praise of God, thanksgiving for some benefit or another, or perhaps petition, recognizing one's need for God in a particular context. Thus, biblical scholar Barnabas Lindars writes, "We find [miracle as a divine act] in the Book of Exodus, but this is not because it is primarily an historical writing, but because it is the cult legend, which is solemnly recited in the national festival. So, too, the remarkable deliverances of Israel at times of national crisis are told from the point of view of salvation-history, and consequently show a tendency to emphasize the miraculous character of the events."[14] Lindars differentiates miraculous events that occur in the cultic narrative of salvation history, the context that accentuates such events, from the more sober even if theologically interpretative events of history beginning with the struggle between Saul and David. "From now on we are in the age when records begin to be kept. The historical narrative attains a high standard of objectivity. This is still true in the case of the Books of Kings, although the work is written from a definite theological standpoint as a sacred history." He goes on to point out that the postexilic historical books, for example, Ezra–Nehemiah and the Books of Maccabees, "continue to be notably free from reports of miracles."[15]

If we take seriously the lines of thinking exemplified above, then we do not approach the Books of Exodus and Joshua from a strictly historiographical point of view. The obvious purpose of the miraculous traditions associated with Moses and Joshua has to do with God's protective presence with his chosen people, what Gerald O'Collins refers to as "the powerful kindness of their God." For that reason, it seems prudent to conclude with John L. McKenzie: "It seems methodologically superior to renounce any effort at exact analysis of the events and of their miraculous character in the strict sense of the term; the traditions do not afford the evidence. The emphasis in the traditions falls not upon the 'miraculous' character of the events, but upon the 'wonder' of the power and will of Yahweh to save."[16]

ELIJAH AND ELISHA

The second set of miracle stories comes from the Elijah–Elisha cycles. Elijah and Elisha probably presided over prophetic-ecstatic coenobitic groups, the "sons of the prophets." The narratives concerning Elijah and Elisha in the Books of Kings stand out in terms of miraculous stories in the Old Testament. Old Testament scholars in their commentaries and monographs uniformly point out the complexity of the narratives when it comes to their interpretation. For example, the author of the article on miracle in Xavier Léon-Dufour's *Dictionary of Biblical Theology* has this to say: "The substantial historicity of the cycles of Elijah and Elisha makes good use of popular exaggerations (2 Kings 1:9–16), which from one cycle to the other grow in extension and frequently lose in religious quality (2 Kings 2:23–24; 6:1–7)."[17] The miracle stories certainly reflect what must be popular exaggerations, and they do lose in terms of religious quality, but perhaps their overriding point is clear enough—that is, that God and his two spokesmen are more religiously authentic than the antics of Baal and his prophets and the various political players in the narrative. "Prophecy stands as a counterforce to the monarchy: whereas the king can summon troops (and the prophets of Baal) to do his bidding, the prophet's power is expressed through the word received from the Lord and, when demonstration of its validity is required, through signs and wonders."[18] This is borne out immediately in the meaning of their names. *Elijah* means in Hebrew "my God is Yah(weh)," and *Elisha* means "my God is salvation." The "miraculous" stories as much as the very names of the prophets themselves are in service to this Yahwistic theological insight and conviction. It is the reality and power of Yahweh above all else to which Elijah and Elisha witness. Barnabas Lindars writes, "Whether [the miracle stories concerning Elijah and Elisha] have been built-up from purely natural happenings or not, they have been remembered and valued because they give vivid expression to the powerful impression which the prophets' personalities made on their contemporaries."[19]

In fact, the Elijah–Elisha cycle is part and parcel of a royal succession narrative, at this point the history of the house of Omri (1 Kings 16:17—2 Kings 11:20). "It is a succession-narrative, told from the point of view of the Yahwistic party at Jerusalem. It is thus hardly surprising that the compiler drew on legends of the prophets to give facts and color to what would otherwise have been a very bare sketch."[20] There can be little doubt that these colorful and popular narratives about miraculous events bring to life what is very much a tedious historiographical—though written from a theological perspective—narrative of ancient Israel. At the same time, one naturally wants to know what to make of these miraculous events attributed to Elijah and Elisha.

Elijah is from Gilead on the east side of the Jordan, and Elisha appears to have been associated with the "sons of the prophets" (2 Kgs 2:3; 4:1, 38; 6:1; 9:1 [ESV]). Likely the collection of the Elijah–Elisha cycle comes from the initiative of Elisha himself or one of his disciples. The Elijah cycle of miracles begins with the three miracles connected with the drought in the reign of King Ahab. The ultimate religious backdrop to the cycle is the struggle between Yahwism and Baalism, the saving God of the Israelites and the fertility god of the Canaanites.

First is the story in 1 Kings 17:2–7 in which Elijah is fed by ravens in the wilderness, a story that bears a family resemblance to the story of Israel in the wilderness, miraculously fed by Yahweh (Exod 16:8–12):

> The word of the LORD came to [Elijah], saying, "Go from here and turn eastward, and hide yourself by

> the Wadi Cherith, which is east of the Jordan. You shall drink from the wadi, and I have commanded the ravens to feed you there." So he went and did according to the word of the LORD; he went and lived by the Wadi Cherith, which is east of the Jordan. The ravens brought him bread and meat in the morning, and bread and meat in the evening; and he drank from the wadi. But after a while the wadi dried up, because there was no rain in the land.[21]

Lindars is surely correct in concluding that, whatever this event means, it lies outside genuine historiographical inquiry and ultimately depends on "personal (and presumably subjective) telling by the subject himself, and may be no more than his way of recounting his experience."[22]

The other two of the three miracles in 1 Kings 17 concern the widow of Zarephath. Zarephath was a town of Sidon, and so it would have been understood to owe its territorial religious allegiance to Baal, not Yahweh. But Elijah is Yahweh's man and mediates Yahweh's power. Elijah prophesies to the woman that her food, the meal and oil, will not run out while the drought continues. Subsequently the widow's son dies or, at least, appears to—"his illness was so severe that there was no breath left in him" (1 Kgs 17:17). Elijah lays the boy on his own bed and stretches over him three times, and as a result the boy is restored to life. Lindars is aware of naturalistic explanations of these two miracles. He knows, for example, of the Scottish Old Testament scholar John Gray's hypothesis that the generosity of the widow toward Elijah was recognized by her neighbors who, touched by her extraordinary generosity in difficult circumstances, took responsibility for continuing to supply her with meal and oil. Lindars comments, "One can hardly resist the impression that the theory…is merely a device to save the historicity of the incident without straining credulity too far."[23] The theological point behind the story of the boy's resuscitation or revivification is the power of Yahweh operating through Elijah who is full of Yahweh's spirit. As a result, the widow, who because of her geographical-political location owes religious allegiance to Baal, now confesses faith in Yahweh: "So the woman said to Elijah, 'Now I know that you are a man of God, and that the word of the LORD in your mouth is truth'" (1 Kgs 17:24).[24] The miracle confirms the meaning of Elijah's name, literally in Hebrew "My God (Eli) is Yah(weh)." Nonetheless, Lindars concludes that the miracle story is really folklore. The folkloric interpretation of the miracle is given further substance according to Lindars when we proceed to read "the very same motifs...in the Elisha cycle."[25]

The next miracle for Elijah is the fire from heaven in his contest with the prophets of Baal on Mount Carmel in 1 Kings 18, an ordeal that seems to reflect what today might be called a rainmaking ceremony. Lindars concludes, "Seen in this light, the whole episode is a trial of strength between the Baal worshipers and the Yahweh worshipers, turning on the success of the rain-making ceremony. It wins popular acceptance for Yahweh. The naturalistic interpretation is difficult to resist in this case. It shows Elijah as a most powerful intercessor on a memorable cultic occasion."[26] Elijah's success at the event turns on his drawing the people away from the worship of Baal toward Yahweh. Here also there is a family resemblance between what happens with Elijah on Mount Carmel and what happened with Moses on Mount Sinai (Exod 24:4–8).

What are we to make of the magnificent story of Elijah's experience on Mount Horeb in 1 Kings 19? En route he is fed by an angel, probably reflecting the motif of 1 Kings 17:3–7, and then there is the wind, the earthquake, the fire, and "a sound of sheer silence" (1 Kgs 19:12). Lindars insightfully comments, "Most readers take this to mean apprehension of God through inner experience, rather than through spectacular phenomena, and this is surely right. The narrative has a poetic quality which forbids literal interpretation."[27]

Finally, with respect to Elijah, we come to the story of his ascension into heaven in 2 Kings 2. A series of wondrous events is recounted. Like the experience of the people of Israel in the Book of Exodus and the Red Sea, the waters of the Jordan are parted by the mantle of Elijah (2 Kgs 2:6–8). It is almost as if Elijah is recapitulating in himself the wondrous saving events of the past, thus emphasizing the constancy and faithfulness of God with his people, "the powerful kindness of God." Lindars reports the interpretation of the Old Testament scholar H. J. Kraus in which this parting of the waters of the Jordan is seen as "a rite in the amphictyonic sacrament at Gilgal commemorating the Exodus, a liturgical act for which the cultic narrative is preserved in Joshua 4."[28] Joshua 4, of course, narrates the passage of the people of Israel dry shod through the parted waters of the river Jordan before they enter the promised land. The "cultic feel" of the Red Sea event in the Book of Exodus, this event in Joshua 4, and the event of 2 Kings 2 is very persuasive indeed, even if it is not quite possible to identify what precise liturgical rite lies behind them. Elisha asks his master for a double portion of his spirit. Then Elijah is taken up by a chariot of fire and horses of fire into heaven (2 Kgs 2:11–12). However the details of these miraculous events are to be interpreted, they have "a deeper purpose than recording marvels in order to impress the credulous." Lindars is surely right in concluding that "they express the great significance which was attached to Elisha's position as Elijah's successor in popular thought."[29]

As with the Elijah cycle, the Elisha cycle contains a series of miracle stories from 2 Kings 2:19—8:6, minus chapter 3.

It has been plausibly suggested that this catena of miracle stories emanates from the oral tradition of various prophetic-ecstatic groups. "It therefore makes sense to propose that these brief miracle stories originated within such groups, each of which recounted, no doubt with advantages, its own version of the strange and memorable deeds of the master."[30] That is how folk memory or community memory works in developing further the identity of the social group around pivotal actions or events attributed to the central characters or personalities of the group.

Elisha purifies the water of an unnamed town, traditionally identified as Jericho, with salt (2:19–22). It has been suggested that the use of salt in this context "probably corresponds to a type of well-attested homeopathic magic."[31] In the face of what is literally an unexplainable and indeed impossible event, this is as good an explanation as one is likely to find. Some insolent boys are torn apart by bears (2:23–25). "[Elisha] went up from there to Bethel; and while he was going up on the way, some small boys came out of the city and jeered at him, saying, 'Go away, baldhead! Go away, baldhead!' When he turned around and saw them, he cursed them in the name of the LORD. Then two she-bears came out of the woods and mauled forty-two of the boys. From there he went on to Mount Carmel, and then returned to Samaria." To say the least, this is a very strange event. Luke Timothy Johnson in fact calls it "an example of true prophetic pettiness."[32] However, there may be a way of interpreting the event that makes it more intelligible, even if not more morally acceptable. Elisha may be understood as the patriarch or abbot of the "sons of the prophets" (see the use of "father" in 2 Kgs 2:12; 13:14), a group of ecstatic prophets living together. The point has been made that the Hebrew word here rendered "boys" is *nearim,* a word that is also used for disciples of prophets. For example, it is used of Gehazi the disciple of Elisha. Similarly, the word translated "small" is *qetanim,* which can also mean "young." Putting these philological possibilities together leads Old Testament scholar Joseph Blenkinsopp persuasively—for me at least—to the following conclusion: "We could perhaps interpret the mockery as rejection of Elisha's leadership by younger members of the Bethel prophetic-ecstatic conventicle who were determined to prevent him visiting them."[33]

Elisha Purifies a Poisoned Pot (4:38–41)

> When Elisha returned to Gilgal, there was a famine in the land. As the company of prophets was sitting before him, he said to his servant, "Put the large pot on, and make some stew for the company of prophets." One of them went out into the field to gather herbs; he found a wild vine and gathered from it a lapful of wild gourds, and came and cut them up into the pot of stew, not knowing what they were. They served some from the men to eat. But while they were eating the stew, they cried out, "O man of God, there is death in the pot!" They could not eat it. He said, "Then bring some flour." He threw it into the pot, and said, "Serve the people and let them eat." And there was nothing harmful in the pot.

It is possible that the gourds may have been the herb colocynth. Lindars thinks that this may have been something "to make the mixture potent to work up prophetic frenzy," but both he and Blenkinsopp also recognize with a degree of humor that this particular herb is a powerful laxative.[34]

Elisha Feeds One Hundred Men with Twenty Loaves (4:42–44)

> A man came from Baal-shalishah, bringing food from the first fruits to the man of God: twenty loaves of barley and fresh ears of grain in his sack. Elisha said, "Give it to the people and let them eat." But his servant said, "How can I set this before a hundred people?" So he repeated, "Give it to the people, and let them eat, for thus says the LORD, 'They shall eat and have some left.'" He set it before them, they ate, and had some left, according to the word of the LORD.

The "people" here are most likely the "sons of the prophets" with whom Elisha was associated.

The cure of Naaman the leprous Syrian (chapter 5) widens the Yahwist perspective of Elisha by opening out Yahweh's power, "the powerful kindness of the God of Israel," to a Gentile. After his being healed from leprosy in the river Jordan, the Syrian takes two bags of Yahweh's territory/soil back to Syria so that he may continue to worship Yahweh in something of Yahweh's domain, in the conviction that the power of a deity is limited to some particular region.[35]

Elisha Makes an Ax Head Float (6:1–7)

> Now the sons of the prophets said to Elisha, "See, the place where we dwell under your charge is too small for us. Let us go to the Jordan and each of us get there a log, and let us make a place for us to dwell there." And he answered, "Go." Then one of them said, "Be pleased to go with your servants." And he answered, "I will go." So he went with them. And when they came to the Jordan, they cut

> down trees. But as one was felling a log, his axe head fell into the water; and he cried out, "Alas, my master! It was borrowed." Then the man of God said, "Where did it fall?" When he showed them the place, he cut off a stick, and threw it in there, and made the iron float. And he said, "Take it up." So he reached out his hand and took it. (ESV)

The comments offered by Barnabas Lindars here may be somewhat tongue-in-cheek but are nonetheless on target: "[Elisha] does this apparently by poking about in the river with a stick, and perhaps guiding it to the brink where it can be reached by hand. If so, it is not really a miracle at all, but this impression has been built up because the man of God was so clever. Faith in his sagacity was justified."[36]

A Woman Recovers Her Inheritance (8:1–6) through the Agency of Elisha and His Servant Gehazi

Finally, a dead man is revived in connection with Elisha's bones (13:20–21). This last miracle story is particularly interesting. In 2 Kings 13:20–21 we read of this miracle occurring:

> So Elisha died, and they buried him. Now bands of Moabites used to invade the land in the spring of the year. As a man was being buried, a marauding band was seen and the man was thrown into the grave of Elisha; as soon as the man touched the bones of Elisha, he came to life and stood on his feet.

Stories like this, relating the power of relics, as it were, are probably nothing more than superstition. "They simply attest the wonder that surrounds a holy man in popular memory, and invite the critic to classify them as folk-lore."[37] Lindars,

I believe, is correct here at the level of historiographical understanding. At the same time and in line with comments already made in this chapter, there is a profound theological conviction at work, expressed in the words of Luke Timothy Johnson: "Whether in public or private, whether for good or for ill, the portrayals of Elijah and Elisha connect in the closest possible fashion the prophetic word and the working of signs and wonders."[38] God is present and active in the ministry of Elijah and Elisha—in the words they speak on behalf of God and in the "signs and wonders" that confirm and validate God's presence and activity through them.

THE BOOK OF TOBIT AND THE BOOK OF DANIEL

The third cycle of miracle stories, if we may call it that, comes from the Books of Tobit and Daniel. We find a number of what might be called "miniature miracles" in the Book of Tobit, a text written about 200 BCE. According to the narrative, Tobit was a man of the tribe of Naphtali who was captured and taken to Assyria when King Shalmaneser destroyed the city of Samaria in 722 BC (see 2 Kgs 17:1–6). He remained true to his ancestral religious values, including the dietary laws, and refused to eat the food of the Gentiles. As he conducted business in Media for the king with whom he found some favor, Tobit left ten talents of silver on deposit in that country. He fell out of favor with the king, however, and had to flee, and as a result lost all of his property. Misfortune continued for Tobit. Bird droppings fell into his eyes and he became blind. He prayed for death. At the same time, a young woman named Sarah, who was the daughter of Raguel, a kinsman of Tobit, was also praying for death. Sarah had been married seven times and each one of her husbands had been killed by a demon before the marriage was consummated. Tobit's and Sarah's prayers for death are answered not as they wished, but with the sending of the angel Raphael to heal them.

This is how the healing happens. Tobit remembers the money he had on deposit and sends his son Tobias to bring it back. Tobias is accompanied by the angel Raphael, who is disguised as a man. While they're en route to Media to recover the money, a large fish from the river Tigris attacks Tobias. Raphael instructs the young man to catch the fish, cut it open, take out its innards, and keep them for medicinal purposes. Raphael also directs Tobias to the house of Raguel and encourages the young man to marry the seven-times-widowed Sarah, especially since Tobias is her next of kin. He is reluctant but the marriage takes place. Tobias does not die because he uses the odoriferous fish's liver and heart to miraculously repel the demon who had been responsible for the deaths of Sarah's husbands. Tobias recovers his father's money and returns home. Raphael instructs him to apply the fish's remaining innards to his father's blind eyes, and miraculously his sight is restored.

This entertaining tale, upholding traditional family and religious values, is an exquisite piece of folklore, enhanced by the "miniature miracles." John J. Collins describes the Book of Tobit in these words: "All these folkloric elements are woven together by a master storyteller with a good sense of humor. What other Israelite hero is undone by bird droppings?... Tobit gives a rare glimpse of popular Jewish piety in the Second Temple period. This involved a lively faith in angels and demons and in cures that we would regard as superstitious, or even magical."[39]

There are two miraculous accounts of salvation from imminent danger in the Book of Daniel, in chapters 3 and 6. In chapter 3, three devout Jews, Shadrach, Meshach, and

Abednego, are thrown into a raging furnace by King Nebuchadnezzar, and they are miraculously delivered from death because of their faithfulness to their ancestral Judaism. "The confrontation between the king and the three Jews anticipates a genre of martyr story that becomes common from the time of the Maccabees onward."[40] In chapter 6 of the book, the hero is Daniel who is thrown into a den of lions and miraculously emerges unscathed. John Collins is surely right in describing these narratives, including the miraculous escapes, in these terms: "The tales in Daniel 1—6 have been aptly said to present 'a lifestyle for the Diaspora.' Their message to the Jews in exile is twofold: participate in the life of the Gentile world and be loyal to the king, but realize that your ultimate success depends on your fidelity to your God and his laws."[41] Probably, then, the purpose of the Book of Daniel is to provide consolation and encouragement in the faith for the Jews during the persecution of Antiochus IV Epiphanes (ca. 215–164 BCE), in pursuit of his program of uniform Hellenization throughout his realm.

Returning by way of conclusion to the commentary offered on these accounts in the Books of Tobit and Daniel by Barnabas Lindars, he says that "the miracles in the story of Tobit and in the early chapters of Daniel...are tendentious folk-tales rather than historical reporting,"[42] wisdom literature in edifying stories rather than history in any serious sense of the word. Written probably around 200 BCE, the Book of Tobit is primarily didactic, a family tale that is meant both to build up family values and perhaps also to entertain.

THE WISDOM OF SOLOMON

The consensus on the Book of Wisdom is that it was composed in Alexandria sometime during the first century BCE.

It probably shares with the apocalyptic literature the aim of encouraging faithful Jews during times of persecution and of warning apostates of the consequences of their choice. However, in contrast with apocalyptic literature that sees the future in this-worldly terms, the Book of Wisdom sees the future in other-worldly terms, "of immortality of the soul and spiritual rewards and punishments after death, but all on the basis of what has happened and is happening in this world."[43] "Wisdom" is personified in chapters 6—10 as a way of talking about God's presence and action in the world. Thus, for example, we read,

> For she [Wisdom] is a breath of the power of
>   God,
> and a pure emanation of the glory of the
>   Almighty;
> therefore nothing defiled gains entrance into her.
> For she is a reflection of eternal light,
> a spotless mirror of the working of God,
> and an image of his goodness.
> Although she is but one, she can do all things,
> and while remaining in herself, she renews all
>   things;
> in every generation she passes into holy souls
> and makes them friends of God, and prophets;
> for God loves nothing so much as the person who
>   lives with wisdom. (Wis 7:25–28)

"The last chapter of the *Wisdom of Solomon* contains a theory of miracles phrased in the scientific terms of the day which...is unique in the biblical literature."[44] The theory essentially maintains that the harmony of the universe has been rearranged for the protection of God's holy people. Miracles represent the harmony of the universe being rearranged. They are not breaches of the laws of nature. In Wisdom 19:6, we read,

> For the whole creation in its nature was fashioned
> anew,
> complying with your commands,
> so that your children might be kept unharmed.

Creation was fashioned anew through the marvelous/miraculous events of the Book of Exodus.[45]

Creation in Genesis	Miracle in Exodus
Darkness covered the waters (1:2)	The cloud covered the camp (14:19–20)
Dry land came from the primeval waters (1:9–10)	Dry land appeared out of the Red Sea (14:21–22)
The land brought forth animals (1:24)	The land brought forth gnats (8:16–19)
Fish in the waters (1:20)	Frogs in the waters (8:2–3)
Birds appeared (1:20)	A new bird appeared from the sea (16:13)

The miraculous for the author of the Book of Wisdom occurs against the background of a rational explanation of reality, but a rational explanation of reality that redounds to the glory of Judaism and its God. In that sense, its rational explanation of the miraculous is finally a work of theological or perhaps more accurately "apologetic" propaganda for the cause of Judaism.

CONCLUSION

To say the least, the element of the miraculous, in the narrower sense of the word, is not a very prominent theme in the Old Testament, as contrasted, for example, with the gospel traditions in the New Testament. A compelling, if not watertight, case can be made that such miraculous actions are there to point to God's providential love for the people of Israel, "the powerful kindness of God," remembered and celebrated in the liturgy. The miraculous is to be understood as expressive of God's presence and power, in word and in action. Finally, the miracle stories found in the Elijah–Elisha cycle and in the Books of Tobit and Daniel, although not exactly identical in intentionality, are best thought of as encouragement to faith in Yahweh alone (Elijah–Elisha) or, in a much later time of Hellenization, as encouragement to faithfulness in periods of persecution.

CHAPTER 3

THE HEALING JESUS

A modern philosophical understanding of reality is not to be assumed as one hundred percent correct and normative for what might have been.

Raymond E. Brown, SS[1]

It is reasonable to think that [Jesus], as well as his followers, saw his miracles as testifying to his being a true messenger from or agent of God.

E. P. Sanders[2]

The miraculous element in the Gospel tradition need not be denied outright, but it has certainly been exaggerated, and needs to be treated with agnostic reserve. What we must look for is the Jesus whose life so deeply impressed his contemporaries, and seek to grasp the meaning of his message and the significance of his person for the salvation of the world.

Barnabas Lindars[3]

INTRODUCTION

This chapter opens with statements from three prominent New Testament scholars, Raymond E. Brown, E. P. Sanders, and Barnabas Lindars. In the statement from Raymond E. Brown we are offered a careful segue into an exploration of the miracles of Jesus. In my reading of Brown's statement, he suggests that it would be improper, without important theological and methodological qualifications, to let a modern philosophical/scientific point of view determine what did and what did not happen in the life of Jesus Christ. We have already recognized this problem in the last chapter on miracles in the Old Testament. Quite simply, if we operate with a modern philosophical/scientific viewpoint, we will misunderstand what the Scriptures are saying. In the statement from E. P. Sanders, operating largely from a historiographical point of view, we are offered a careful historical conclusion: that is, from a historical point of view, Jesus and his followers viewed his miraculous activity as somehow divinely confirmed or endorsed. When Barnabas Lindars, the Anglican Franciscan and biblical scholar, speaks about "agnostic reserve" with reference to the miracle stories concerning Jesus, he is not endorsing agnosticism as such. If anything, what he has to say is rooted in the whole incarnational event of Jesus Christ, in anyone's book from any perspective something that is most impressive indeed. This deep impression of Jesus's identity and mission, implies Lindars, should not rest exclusively on the tradition of the miracle stories, nor should it be reduced to them. Lindars's point of view seems very balanced indeed. Could we say that Jesus himself, the incarnation, is *the* miracle? If that seems reasonable, then it may follow that the very existence of Christianity itself may share in the miraculous. Think of these words from Luke Timothy Johnson:

> In similar fashion, the stunning "sign and wonder" of earliest Christianity is its very existence in the world of the Roman Empire. How improbable it was that the brief ministry of a failed Jewish messiah executed by the state should give rise to a movement whose communities, largely Gentile in makeup, would spread across the Mediterranean world within a period of forty years! In the case of Jesus and the rise of Christianity, the gap between ostensible cause and consequent effect is so great as to demand being termed a "wonder," a manifestation of God's presence and power in creation.[4]

This wider and broader understanding of the miraculous, of God's presence and power in creation, promises a more rewarding starting point for thinking about individual accounts of miracle. It reflects what Johnson has called his wider "believing" hermeneutic of generosity and charity disclosing God's presence and power.

> In sum, the earliest writings from the Christian movement claim the experience of God's presence and power, not just generally in creation, but specifically in the new creation in which they participate; not as discrete events in the past, but as the condition of their continuing existence. In the sense that I have described the miraculous, all these claims are miraculous in character: they attribute everything happening to them to God's agency.... The miraculous is not occasional or accidental in earliest Christianity: the miraculous forms the very substance of Christianity's being in the world.[5]

To say the least, the sheer volume of research and published work on the historical Jesus, including the miracles attributed to him, is overwhelming and necessarily requires a very selective reading. That is what I attempt in this and the next chapter regarding the miracles of Jesus. John P. Meier, one of the foremost respected questers of the historical Jesus, writes,

> In the ["history of religion" school] the claim is usually made that reports of Jesus' miracles reflect the literary forms, themes, and motifs found in pagan and Jewish miracle stories circulating in the Mediterranean world around the turn of the era. There is a great deal of truth to this claim, but at the same time some distinctions are in order. A proper evaluation of pagan, Jewish, and Gospel miracle stories must involve respect for differences as well as similarities.[6]

Taking seriously what Meier has said, it will be helpful before looking at the gospel miracles to turn briefly to miraculous activity in Jewish circles and then in the Greco-Roman world.

JUDAISM: GALILEAN CHARISMATIC HOLY MEN

Consider this statement by Barnabas Lindars: "Many of the healing miracles would hardly be regarded as miracles if they had been seen by modern observers, whose presuppositions are so different from first-century Galilee, and could be credited to other healers and exorcists of the time equally well." So far, so good. What Lindars is saying is a statement of fact. However, he goes on to make some further comments that are particularly interesting:

> The fact that they are mostly set in Galilee is not without importance. The people of Galilee were of mixed stock, though they had been largely Judaized under John Hyrcanus (135–105 BC). In New Testament times they were noted for their credulousness and their enthusiasms. After the fall of Jerusalem (AD 70) the rabbis tend to discountenance emphasis on miracles, classing Christians with Galileans in this respect. The gospel passages in which numerous miracles are summarized (Mark 3:7–12, etc.) are typical of the sort of exaggeration to which these people were prone.[7]

So, Lindars is telling us that there were holy Galilean men in the first century AD about whom miracle stories were told. That is simply a fact. It is equally a fact that there were Gentile pagans about whom miracle stories were told. Historiographical and theological competence demands that both these facts be not only acknowledged but examined, albeit not in detail. Let us turn first to Jewish examples, Honi the Circle-Drawer and Hanina ben Dosa. Since this material is largely unfamiliar to most Christians, the following description accompanied by some texts will help, not least in providing a somewhat fuller picture of Galilean Judaism at the time of Jesus.

There was a first-century BC Jewish holy man, or *hasid*, named Honi the Circle-Drawer in rabbinic circles, named as Onias the Righteous by the Jewish historian Josephus. It is possible that he came from the Galilee.[8] Sometime before the fall of Jerusalem to the Roman Pompey in 63 BC, Honi was requested to pray for rain, and as a result of his petition, God miraculously caused a great downpour.[9]

While it is possible that Honi was Galilean, it is certain that Hanina, another Jewish charismatic, came from Galilee from the town of Arav, located about six miles north of Sepphoris, the capital city of Galilee. This would put it about ten miles north of Nazareth. There is some consensus that Hanina flourished before the fall of Jerusalem in AD 70, and perhaps even afterward, and that he had been for a time a disciple of Rabbi Yohanan ben Zakkai. He was addressed as "Rabbi," just as Jesus was. Some accounts of miracles from the Babylonian Talmud or later sources are associated with Hanina, and the biblical scholar Joseph Blenkinsopp offers a detailed account of seven such miracle stories.[10]

Géza Vermes, the Jewish scholar and expert on the Dead Sea Scrolls and on Galilean Judaism, finds it puzzling that New Testament scholars do not make more of these Galilean holy men/*hasidim* when dealing with Jesus.[11] Alluding to the work of Géza Vermes, Blenkinsopp writes, "As Vermes noted, we have in the words and deeds of Hanina some of the makings of a gospel, of course without a martyrdom or passion narrative."[12] After his examination of Honi and Hanina, Vermes reaches this conclusion: "For all the precautions imperative to a thesis which, owing to the nature of the sources, must in part remain hypothetical, coincidence cannot reasonably be invoked to account for all the similarities....It would appear, rather, that the logical inference must be that the person of Jesus is to be seen as part of first-century charismatic Judaism and as the paramount example of the early *Hasidim* or Devout."[13] It is helpful from a historical point of view with Vermes to view Jesus as a devout Galilean *hasid*/holy man, and as one who could perform miracles. Jesus's teaching and the consequent understandings of his person as divine in the earliest Christian communities, however, were not only far more extensive than any of his peer Galilean *hasidim* but also gave rise to a profound renewal movement within Judaism that developed into the Christian church. The similarities between the stories told of the Galilean holy men/miracle workers and Jesus may be readily admitted. From the earliest days of Christianity, however, Jesus was understood to be divine, not with the clarity of the Nicene *homoousios*/consubstantial formula in the wake of the Arian controversy, but tending in its direction.[14] Take, for example, the testimony of St. Paul, the earliest Christian writer. Paul shows no real interest in the miraculous activity of Jesus for its own sake. Rather, his encounter with the risen Jesus brought him to an understanding of Jesus that can be described only as situating Jesus within what we might call "the orbit of the divine." As one scholar has put it recently, "A total revolution of values is being produced in [Paul's] life. Paul feels himself as 'a new person.' His own transformation is the best testimony to what he has experienced. From his own experience he can proclaim to all: 'it is no longer I who live, but it is Christ who lives in me.'"[15] Without getting into christological apologetics, it is preeminently clear that much more, so much more, is going on in the entirety of the Jesus-event, including without exaggerating the miracle stories, than in the accounts of his holy Galilean countrymen, whatever degree of historicity may be attributed to them.

MIRACLES IN THE GRECO-ROMAN WORLD

It is amply verifiable that "both miracle and magic were 'in the air' as Jesus began his ministry and performed extraordinary deeds deemed by some to be miraculous."[16] This is the case not only in first-century Judaism but also in Greco-Roman society.

John Meier points out in terms of the concept "magic," that already in antiquity it had a negative connotation and also that in modernity there is no agreed definition of *magic* from the scholars in the various disciplines—sociology, anthropology, history, and so on. He also recognizes that among a certain cohort of scholars, "magic" describes the folkloric side of popular religiosity in contrast with the more rationalized and enlightened religion of the few. With these methodological observations and cautions in mind, Meier makes the decision to contrast the miracle stories in the Gospels with magical papyri from the ancient world to differentiate the two.

The Greco-Roman magical papyri date from the second or first century BC to the fifth century AD. In these papyri we find words are multiplied, divine titles and names are registered in litanies, and various kinds of ritual strategies are offered to combat all manner of human ailments and challenges. "The desired effects of magic rituals in the papyri range from the serious and beneficent goal of exorcism, through the relatively pedestrian or self-centered goals of winning a horse race, obtaining money, curing a runny nose, exterminating bedbugs, obtaining a lover, or achieving an erection, to the sinister purpose of doing harm to another, especially a rival in business, love, or legal action."[17] While it is true that some of the miracle stories in the Gospels seem to demonstrate magical characteristics—for example, the story of the woman with the hemorrhage who touches Jesus's garment and is healed in Mark 5:24–34—this is the exception rather than the rule. Even in this quasi-magical account, ultimately the emphasis is on the faith of the woman: "[Jesus] said to her, 'Daughter, your faith has made you well; go in peace, and be healed of your disease'" (v. 34). The litanies and the registers of divine names and words in the papyri, the accumulation of which was supposed to render the magical outcome more powerful and more likely, have no real parallel in the gospel tradition.

Having made this distinction between magic and miracle, Meier very helpfully goes on to enumerate six characteristics of miraculous activity, especially that of Jesus recorded in the Gospels.[18] First, the normal context for a miracle is a relationship of faith/trust/love between the subject and Jesus. Second, the subject normally makes a request of Jesus, although sometimes Jesus himself takes the initiative, but there is never any question of a business transaction along the lines of the magical papyri. Third, the miracle occurs with just a few words uttered by Jesus and occasionally a symbolic gesture—one thinks especially, for example, of the use of spittle in Mark 7:33. Fourth, there is no element whatsoever of coercion between the subject and Jesus—"A basic supposition of the gospel miracle stories is that God's hand is not to be forced." Fifth, the miracles of Jesus are understood within the context of the kingdom of God, of which they are signs and symbols. Sixth, "Jesus' miracles do not directly punish or hurt anyone." This stands in clear contrast with some of the requests made in the magical papyri.

THE MIRACLES OF JESUS

Barnabas Lindars points out that "because of the circumstances in which the oral tradition was formed we cannot expect to get to the bottom of all the miracle-stories."[19] In this comment he is acknowledging what is really commonplace, that is, that prior to the Gospels and to any possible written sources that may lie behind them, the traditions concerning Jesus were passed on by word of mouth. Lindars continues, "Memory is fickle. Although the use of much of the tradition in the missionary and catechetical work of the church…and no doubt in the liturgy too, ensured that the theological interpretation remained central, some of it at any rate can have had little more than hagiographical interest."[20] Furthermore, conceding something to Lindars's point, even if a biblical scholar concluded that the miracles ascribed to Jesus of Nazareth in the Gospels were historically probable, that judgment in itself would not necessarily mean that they were, theologically speaking, "miracles," that is to say, immediately and directly acts of God beyond what was possible for human beings. Such a judgment goes beyond the competence of a historian. At most, the historian may judge that the sources critically examined yield a result of possibility or probability regarding the historicity of the miracle stories.

It is clearly the case in the Gospels of the New Testament—the apocryphal Gospels are a different problem altogether[21]—that the miracles worked by Jesus are first understood not as demonstrations of his power but rather as expressive of who he is and what he is doing. In that precise sense they are to be understood as primarily christological, inviting deeper insight and commitment to his person. Often, there is a lack of sensationalism in the accounts, and the accounts are actually very sober.

In the New Testament there are seventeen accounts of healing, including three of revivification. There are also six counts of exorcisms and eight nature miracles. What are we to make of these narratives? Right away, one must admit that it would be an extraordinary feat of radical skepticism simply to dismiss these miracle narratives, not least because they are woven in a seemingly integrated fashion into the warp and woof of the gospel narratives. At the same time, it would be very foolish simply to accept these narratives without further ado because, as Alan Richardson (and many other New Testament scholars) has noted, "Miracles were everyday events in an age which knew nothing about the fixity of natural law, and every village had its wonder-worker."[22] Miracles were certainly not regarded as an immediate and incontestable demonstration of divinity, something that would occur much later in Christian apologetics. Recall the passage from the Gospel of St. Mark following the acknowledgment that Jesus exorcised demons and anointed with oil many who were sick, healing them:

> King Herod heard of it, for Jesus' name had become known. Some were saying, "John the baptizer has been raised from the dead; and for this reason these powers are at work in him." But others said, "It is Elijah." And others said, "It is a prophet, like one of the prophets of old." But when Herod heard of it, he said, "John, whom I beheaded, has been raised." (Mark 6:14–16)

What is reported in this passage is a variety of explanations for Jesus's working of miracles. What is not disputed in the passage is that he did so. That is why in Mark 11:27–28 the evangelist goes on to say, "As [Jesus] was walking in the temple, the chief priests, the scribes, and the elders came to him and said, 'By what authority are you doing these things? Who gave you this authority to do them?'" In other words, the chief priests, the scribes, and the elders did not contest the fact that Jesus worked miracles. Their concern had to do with the authority by which he worked them.

JESUS THE HEALER

In the gospel narratives we read about Jesus performing exorcisms and healing people. Luke Timothy Johnson offers some helpful comments about exorcisms and healing.

> In some sense, the distinction between exorcisms and healing is artificial, for both kinds of miracles

> are forms of healing. The distinction has some validity, because the exorcisms so clearly address forms of mental derangement, while the healings concern mainly physical ailments. Yet both demonic possession and physical illness result (especially in a society structured by rules of purity) in the ones so afflicted experiencing isolation and exclusion from normal society. In turn, regaining a full humanity, through liberation from spiritual captivity or physical affliction, means as well regaining a place among other humans.[23]

In his own lifetime it was not only the friends and disciples of Jesus who accepted and noted his healing powers. Those opposed to him also accepted and noted them. Their question, however, was "By whose power did he perform these healings?" (see Matt 12:28; Mark 3:22). Some scholars point out that history, especially ancient history, is peppered with healers. That is not unique to Jesus. Few scholars seriously dispute that Jesus was a source of healing for others. While it is true, as Luke Timothy Johnson insists, that "Christians do not approach the miracles of the Gospels with the eyes of critical historiography, asking which of these reports is accurate and which not, but with the eyes of faith, seeking to understand the meaning of the signs and wonders they narrate," nonetheless questions about the historicity of the healings attributed to Jesus are not unreasonable and are perhaps unavoidable.[24]

SOME RECENT PERSPECTIVES

Hubert Richards, biblical scholar and popular philosopher of religion, asks, "Could it be that all humans possess psychosomatic powers which very few avail themselves of?" Richards is quite emphatic on this point, insisting that the kind of miracles that Jesus worked were the kind of miracles that human beings can work. He cites the logion from John: "Very truly I tell you, the one who believes in me will also do the works that I do and, in fact, will do greater works than these, because I am going to the Father" (14:12).[25]

In contemporary Scriptural scholarship there has been a definite shift away from asking "What actually happened?" to "What does this text or narrative mean?" This is no escapism from the factuality of the events. There is the added recognition that "the actual historical reality standing behind the miracle stories is now lost to us. It is impossible to reconstruct the original photographable event, simply because we only have access to it through the eyes of those who have already imposed their interpretation on it."[26] Having acknowledged this, however, this question of the historicity of the miracle stories in the Gospels is part and parcel of a much larger issue. It raises the question of what is actually at stake in Christian belief. Is Christian belief an expression of the experience of new life or perhaps "authentic existence" at this time? Or does Christian faith entail beliefs about past events and future expectations that cannot be verified in any obviously straightforward way in present human experience?[27] Does the entire event of Jesus Christ have only symbolic power, albeit very real symbolic power with the capacity for real human transformation, or does it refer with all the appropriate, scholarly, critical qualifications to things that actually occurred in the life of the historical Jesus? If symbolic power is not founded on actual events in the life of the historical Jesus, then, to say the least, the credibility of Christianity is enormously undermined. A Christian biblical scholar in the skeptical tradition of Rudolph Bultmann, for example, would believe the miracle stories are powerfully symbolic but nothing more. A more traditional

Christian biblical scholar—indeed, Christians generally—would want to affirm that "the miracles of Jesus are not only signs of the possibility of new life for the Christian era now; they are also signs *and evidence* of Christ's special status and authority to proclaim a state of affairs which is only to be brought into being in the future." Hugo Meynell sums it up judiciously when he says, "The question about miracles which is of importance for traditional Christians is whether the marvelous events alleged in the Gospels, or at least events very like them, actually took place."[28] Meynell is correct. Even though we cannot ascertain with certitude what actually took place behind the miracle accounts of the Gospels, we may agree with the song "Something Good" from *The Sound of Music* that "nothing comes from nothing, nothing ever could." It seems to be a very solid principle, and so we can certainly affirm that behind the healing activity of Jesus something very powerful and noteworthy took place, to say the least.

For Jesus, the healings that were accomplished in and through him were signposts pointing to God's kingdom, the establishment of God's rule in this world. His intention was not for people to get excited and remain in wonder about these healings but rather for people to ask about their own healing, their own blindness and paralysis as it were.

Hubert Richards acknowledges that some who read his viewpoint will contest that he is explaining away the miracles as they have come to understand and love them. In moving away from the question of "happenedness" or historicity, he and those who think like him have dumbed down the miracle stories of the Gospels. While he understands that sort of response, he also insists that his interpretation is much deeper. "It is an invitation to understand [the miracles] more deeply, and to accept a frightening responsibility: we are, each of us, called to work miracles ourselves."[29]

The Anglican New Testament scholar, theologian, and bishop Hugh Montefiore wrote an interesting book with the title *The Miracles of Jesus*.[30] The book is interesting because it approaches the phenomenon of Jesus's miracles from the point of view of parapsychology. Montefiore notes that when he was lecturing on the New Testament at Cambridge, he "tended to vacillate" on the question of Jesus's miracles. As a modern man he encountered difficulties with the historicity of the miracles, that is, until he discovered parapsychology. "It never occurred to me that there might be something paranormal about them, and indeed I would have been laughed out of court by my fellow lecturers and professors had I suggested this."[31] He began to explore the suggestion that Jesus may have had paranormal powers and that this was a much better explanatory hypothesis for the miracles. While he adopts the position of John Meier with respect to the historicity of the miracles and their criteria, he posits the paranormal powers of Jesus as the efficient cause.[32]

Montefiore brings to our attention what he regards as established facts about Jesus and his activity: Jesus showed great powers of insight and intuition; he seems to have known things that were happening at a distance; he seems to have had what would be called today telepathic powers. So, for example, in the pericope in St. John's Gospel about Jesus and the Samaritan woman (John 4:16–18, 29)—although he recognizes there are questions about the historicity of John's Gospel narrative—Montefiore wonders if Jesus's knowledge of this woman expressed in her comment, "Come and see a man who told me everything I have ever done!" is "another instance of his paranormal knowledge."[33] When he comes to the person of Judas in the passion narratives and the apostle's betrayal of Jesus, he asks, "Did Jesus have supernatural knowledge about all things, and therefore about his betrayer, or did he have intuitional knowledge of a telepathic kind which gave him insight into the mind of Judas Iscariot?"[34] Montefiore's book is filled with his speculative comments and interpretations along the spectrum of the paranormal. In the epilogue to his book he recognizes the kinds of objections that may be raised against his line of interpretation. He has shown or, better, attempted to show that parapsychology is not "a bogus enterprise" but an appropriate scholarly discipline. He acknowledges that scholars with other philosophical and theological presuppositions that involve explanations of the miraculous in terms of "myths" will not find his approach helpful since basically he is at least in principle open to the historicity of the miracles. He puts forward "this type of explanation as a fresh possibility to be considered. It is perhaps most likely to commend itself to those who believe that the Gospels are based on historical events and actual sayings, but who find it difficult to accept in many cases a miraculous or supernatural explanation."[35]

There are two values in Montefiore's approach to miracles. First, there is his openness to acknowledging and accepting the historicity of the gospel tradition of Jesus's miracles. In an age in which so much skepticism and suspicion has been poured on the historical worth of the gospel narratives, this is surely a plus. Fully aware of the critical stances, he nonetheless acknowledges the importance of the historical "happenedness" of the miraculous tradition. Second, to say the least, his hypothesis concerning the paranormal is most interesting. The primary difficulty with it is its failure to persuade a consensus of scholars. This may be due to the veneer of charlatanism that surrounds parapsychology. If, in the future, researchers find experiences and understandings of the paranormal to be well-established, Montefiore's hypothesis may gain greater acceptance. But that is a matter for the future.

The back cover of Jeffrey John's *The Meaning in the Miracles* has a comment from John P. Meier, author of a multivolume work on the historical Jesus: "Over the years of writing *A Marginal Jew*, I have had to plow through many books on miracles. This is the first book on miracles I have ever read that actually invites readers to move from exegesis through meditation to prayer. A welcome change indeed!"[36] Meier's exhaustive (and exhausting!) account of the miracles is found in his *A Marginal Jew*, vol. 2, *Mentor, Message and Miracles*.[37] It runs to 1,136 pages, about half of which is devoted to the miracles. His comment on Jeffrey John is, therefore, high praise.

Jeffrey John employs a generous hermeneutic toward the miraculous activity of Jesus. He explicitly goes further than Luke Timothy Johnson, however, in deliberately leading the reader into meditation and prayer and so to the development of the Christian spiritual life. We will make use of many of his insights in our consideration of individual miracles, especially the so-called nature miracles. At this point, attention will be focused on his interpretative principles. In his treatment, fully aware of the range of contemporary approaches, John avoids both credulity and reductionism.

It is certainly true, John believes, that Jesus performed miracles but was cautious about being known simply as a wonderworker. The miracles are both invitations to faith in his person and at the same time signs of the inbreaking of God's kingdom, in which all that ails humankind will be healed. He acknowledges the historicity of Jesus's miraculous activity, but in his judgment the point is missed if our inquiry remains at that level, the level of "what actually happened." The miracles are to be understood as profoundly theological and invitational in a christological direction.

> *All* the gospel miracles of Jesus healing the blind and deaf are to be interpreted in terms of this theology of revelation: their point is not medical but spiritual and theological. Whatever history may

> lie behind the stories of individual healings, their meaning and importance in the evangelists' mind is a universal, symbolic one: these miracles are about the potential of us all to be healed of our age-old, inherited spiritual deafness and blindness.[38]

When it comes to the exorcisms performed by Jesus, John is particularly clear. Recognizing the resistance of modernity vis-à-vis the notion of the demonic and therefore of exorcistic activity, he insists that the gospel understanding of the demonic is "more subtle and profound than the usual alternatives of credulity or skepticism allow."[39] "We are not required to believe in the existence of fork-tailed demons, nor even, necessarily, in the powers as being entirely distinct, self-existent entities."[40] Many will find this a refreshingly straightforward statement. At the same time, John goes on to make more illuminating remarks about the demonic:

> Every organization or community as well as every individual has its corporate "demon"—that is, its spiritual as well as worldly aspect; and its potential for generating good or evil will depend on whether it is ordered according to God's will or against it. All systems and societies are therefore capable of becoming demonic in the worst sense. The past century has seen plenty of political systems whose demonic nature can hardly be gainsaid. The phenomenon of Nazism positively demands the vocabulary of the demonic, as a transcendent spiritual sickness which corporately possessed a people, and we have seen other extreme manifestations of corporate evil in more recent years, in Rwanda and elsewhere.[41]

To say the least, very sane and balanced comments.

Very briefly and to illustrate John's approach to "nature" miracles such as changing water into wine or the feeding of the five thousand, he has this to say:

> If Jesus once turned 120 gallons of water into wine at a country wedding, so what? How does it change me? Or if he once fed five thousand people with a few loaves of bread, what difference does it make to me? But if I realize that these miracles point to a feast with Jesus that I can share in now, to a way in which I can be united with him now through receiving him sacramentally in bread and wine, then the miracle ceases to be a remote event of the past, and becomes part of a personal, joyful experience of Christ's never-failing gift of himself to his church.[42]

CONCLUSION

With the help of contemporary scholarship and the extraordinary amount of research that has gone into the miracle accounts of the Gospels, this chapter has tried to steer a middle course between a thoroughgoing skepticism and a mindless credulity. There can be little doubt that historical-critical approaches to the Scriptures have opened horizons of theological insight. Contemporary approaches have moved away from viewing the miraculous activity ascribed to Jesus as proofs of his divinity, a view that has lasted for centuries. In recognizing the progress made by contemporary scholarship, the very title of Jeffrey John's book *The Meaning in the Miracles* provides the most helpful way forward in understanding the miracles. They are not to be understood in the first place as accurate historiography. They are to be understood as theology, as Christology, inviting both insight and commitment to the person of Jesus. Faith in Jesus necessarily comes into play. At the same time, from a historical point of view it seems historically certain that Jesus of Nazareth, the devout Galilean *hasid*, healed people of various ailments, including what was understood in antiquity to be demonic possession. If, as Christian believers, we would follow the lead of Jeffrey John, then the real faith-point of the miracle stories is this: "What is Jesus saying to me in and through this narrative? What is the meaning *in* the miracle for me?"

CHAPTER 4

THE NATURE MIRACLES

What is acclaimed [in the Bible] as a miracle is anything which reveals the God of surprises, whether it is the star-spangled sky proclaiming the glory of God, or simply a blade of grass which speaks to the believer of God's power.

Hubert J. Richards[1]

Theological motives dominate the narratives as our evangelists have recorded them for us, and it is hardly possible to discover from them "what really happened" as a matter of strict historical fact.

Alan Richardson[2]

The real aim of all the miracle stories—if they are not to be seen as mere wonder-working—is to strengthen and illuminate *faith*: that is, a *relationship* between Christ and the hearer.

Jeffrey John[3]

As we scroll through these *pericopae* on what are called "the nature miracles," we notice a distinction being made between what might be called the historical and the symbolic approaches. The historical approach asks, "Did this miracle actually happen as it is described?" The symbolic approach asks, "What does this miracle mean?" Both approaches can be very problematic. The historical approach, inflexibly applied, leads to a biblical literalism or fundamentalism, and when this happens with the symbolic approach, it may lead us to an unreal Jesus. The living, actual flesh-and-blood Jesus may recede into a subjective symbolism that evaporates his existential reality. Why can't we advocate both the historical *and* the symbolic approaches? Why do we have to decide either-or rather than both-and? The classic posture of Catholic theological methodology is both-and, not either-or. Theologian David Brown puts it like this: "The status of Jesus' miracles is often presented in terms of an either-or: either historical or symbolic. But of course, there is no reason why they should not have been both."[4]

Any decision made about the historicity of these "nature" miracles will necessarily reflect one's philosophical presuppositions and one's assessment of the origin and development of the gospel traditions.

> [The nature miracles] have proved to be the biggest stumbling block for critics through the ages; whereas exorcisms and healings are obviously expressions of compassion and can perhaps even be "explained" in terms of psychosomatic medicine, many readers find these accounts, of stilling storms and walking on water and feeding thousands from scraps of food, to be extravagant, exaggerated, scientifically implausible, and above all arbitrary exercises in power. Closer examination, however, allows

> us to see dimensions of these accounts that are missed when we focus solely on the mechanics of thaumaturgy or the red herring of historicity.[5]

Before moving into these more philosophical issues, let's spend some time looking at the narratives themselves with the help of biblical commentators and scholars.

1. THE CURSING OF THE FIG TREE: MARK 11:12–22 (MATT 21:18–22)

This is the only "destructive" miracle performed by Jesus, and in terms of the cumulative character of Jesus that emerges out of all the Gospels, it certainly seems out of character. New Testament scholar Graham Stanton writes of this miracle, "Since a parable of a barren fig tree is recorded in Luke 13:6–9, the miracle story may have 'grown' out of a parable Jesus told."[6] Perhaps, but it is not really necessary to go that route, argues Jeffrey John.

> The truth is that the gospel writers simply do not make the same clear-cut distinctions that we try to make between what Jesus did and the stories he told. What matters is that in him the promises and prophecies of the Old Testament come true—whether it is in what he says, or does, or is. Mark would not have worried that the act of Jesus withering the fig tree suggested he was petulant or irritable. That kind of novelistic character-portrayal which is normal to us does not come into his thinking. Rather he would have understood Jesus' withering of the tree as a "sign" in the tradition of the Old Testament prophets (*oth* in Hebrew)—that is,

> as an action, which may be "miraculous" or otherwise in terms of the laws of nature, but which enacts the deeper truth that it symbolizes.[7]

What is that deeper truth in this "miraculous" action? It has to do with God visiting his people and finding them without fruit, like Jeremiah 8:13:

> When I wanted to gather them, says the LORD,
> there are no grapes on the vine,
> nor figs on the fig tree;
> even the leaves are withered,
> and what I gave them has passed away from them.

The fig tree is a symbol of the people of Israel, the Jews. "The point of the story is that God has now finally visited his people Israel, that they have failed to bear the fruit that was expected of them, and that therefore from now on they are cursed and doomed to die: 'May no one ever eat fruit from you again.'"[8] Jeffrey John firmly rejects as impossible the notion that Jesus cursed his own people. "It is an idea that is impossible to ascribe to Jesus himself, but which, having arisen as a result of the events of 70 AD, was then further reinforced in 85 AD when Christians were formally expelled from the Jewish synagogues."[9] I find John's understanding very persuasive and, as a result, view this cursing of the fig tree as an expression of the growing animosity toward and alienation of the Christian communities from Judaism and the nation in the latter half of the first century, an animosity and alienation that one sees reflected in the Gospels of St. Matthew and St. John, both of them probably written between AD 80 and 100.

2. THE MIRACULOUS CATCH OF FISH: LUKE 5:1–11 (JOHN 21:4–11)

"Which was the original setting of the story—Luke or John—or what experience underlies it, is now impossible to say."[10] Nonetheless, the meaning of the story has to do with the words, "Do not be afraid; from now on you will be catching people" (Luke 5:10). Here our interest is in the Lukan version of the story. Looking back for its roots into the Old Testament, one finds the words of Ezekiel in 47:9–10, the words describing Ezekiel's vision of the river of life flowing out of the restored temple in Jerusalem and where the catch of plentiful fish is a sign of God's gathering in his people at the end of time: "Wherever the river goes, every living creature that swarms will live, and there will be very many fish, once these waters reach there. It will become fresh; and everything will live where the river goes. People will stand fishing beside the sea from En-gedi to En-eglaim; it will be a place for the spreading of nets; its fish will be of a great many kinds, like the fish of the Great Sea." Jeffrey John notes that "there are examples of early Christian art depicting Peter and John holding a net on either side of a stream flowing from the temple, which show that the Ezekiel reference behind it was not lost on the early church."[11]

3. THE SEA MIRACLES: MARK 4:35–41 (MATT 8:18–27; LUKE 8:22–25); MARK 6:45–52

"The wonders on the water strongly echo Scriptural themes concerning the sea: its association with the primordial chaos over which God exercises creative power, its inherent dangers from which God alone can save (see, e.g., Gen 1:1, 9; Pss 78:13, 53; 89:9; 93:4; 106:9, 22; 136:15; Job 41:1–34). In both stories, the sea is a threatening force to which Jesus proves superior....The power at work in Jesus is God's own power within and over creation."[12]

In talking about the nature miracles, the Anglican scripture scholar and theologian of the mid-twentieth century Alan Richardson offers this very useful comment: "It is worth noting that what may appear to us to be a 'nature miracle' may be an exorcism in first-century belief: Jesus casts out the demon of the storm in Mark 4:35–41 just as he casts the unclean spirits out of demoniacs....The symbolical significance of Christ's Sea-Miracles rests in the last resort upon the imagery of the ancient mythology in which the high God smites 'the deep' (*Tiamat, Tehom,* Gen 1:2; Rahab, Isa 51:9f; Ps 89:9f; Leviathan, Ps 104:26; Job 41:1...)."[13]

Some comments from Jeffrey John are also particularly helpful:

> In later Jewish religion the sea retained its evil associations as the natural abode of demons; rabbinic theology provided for both a "fiery" and a "watery" hell. (This is probably why, in the ceiling of the Gerasene demoniac, the demons end up there, in their proper place.) In the first of these two sea-miracles, when Jesus calms the storm he addresses it as if it were a quasi-personal force. He uses the same word that he used to the demoniac in the synagogue (Mark 1:25)—a curious verb, which means literally "Be muzzled!"—in the way one might subdue a rabid animal. There is some evidence to suggest that the word was already in liturgical use by exorcists to command the "binding"

> of demons. In Mark's mind the coming of the storm shows Jesus' power over the forces of supernatural evil just as clearly as the explicit healing of the possessed. Both miracles show him driving back and "binding" the demonic powers that have invaded the world—two skirmishes in the war which, in Mark's Gospel, begins with the temptation in the wilderness and ends with the triumph of the cross.[14]

Jeffrey John also draws attention to Psalm 107:23–29, which may have given the Mark story "its general shape; and the fact that it refers to a number of ships may well be the reason why Mark's story adds, without any further explanation or follow-up, 'And a number of boats were with him.'"[15] Reproducing the verses of this psalm may be helpful to see the point:

> Some went down to the sea in ships,
>   doing business on the mighty waters;
> they saw the deeds of the LORD,
>   his wondrous works in the deep.
> For he commanded and raised the stormy wind,
>   which lifted up the waves of the sea.
> They mounted up to heaven, they went down to
>   the depths;
>   their courage melted away in their calamity;
> they reeled and staggered like drunkards,
>   and were at their wits' end.
> Then they cried to the LORD in their trouble,
>   and he brought them out from their distress;
> he made the storm be still,
>   and the waves of the sea were hushed.

The second sea miracle has Jesus walking on the water. Turning to some Old Testament texts that may have informed Mark's account here we find the following:
From Isaiah 43:16:

> Thus says the LORD,
> who makes a way in the sea,
> a path in the mighty waters.

From Job 9:8:

> [God] who alone stretched out the heavens
> and trampled the waves of the Sea;
> who made the Bear and Orion,
> the Pleiades and the chambers of the south.

Psalm 77:19:

> Your way was through the sea,
> your path, through the mighty waters;
> yet your footprints were unseen.

In the sea miracle in Mark 6:48 we come across some strange words: "When [Jesus] saw that they were straining at the oars against an adverse wind, he came towards them early in the morning, walking on the sea. He intended to pass them by." Walking toward the disciples, yet intending to pass them by? What does this mean? "It begins to make sense, however, in the light of a number of passages where God reveals himself in 'passing by' his people or his prophets, and especially in Exodus 33:18–19 where Yahweh 'passes by' Moses, and discloses to him his glory and his name."[16] The Exodus passage is particularly illuminating: "Moses said, 'Show me your glory, I pray.' And he said, 'I will make all my goodness pass before you, and will proclaim before you the name, "The LORD"'....And the LORD continued, 'See, there is a place by me where you shall stand on the rock; and while my glory passes by I will put you in a cleft of the rock, and I will cover you with my hand until I have passed by'" (33:18–19, 21–22). This puts a whole new twist on Jesus intending to pass by. Consider the following words from the Markan passage: "But when they saw him walking on the sea, they thought it was a ghost and cried out; for they all saw him and were terrified. But immediately he spoke to them and said, 'Take heart, it is I; do not be afraid'" (6:49–50). Those words translated into English as "it is I" are very powerfully revealing words in Greek. In Greek literally they read, "Take heart, I am [*ego eimi*]; do not be afraid." The words are especially revealing, as Jeffrey John comments: "Here, no less than in John's Gospel—but much more hidden—Jesus is himself seen to be none other than Yahweh, the great I AM, the source and end of all that is."[17] This understanding grounds the narrative in a profound and deep Christology.

Turning yet again to Jeffrey John for succinct comment: "When Mark gives us the chorus of the disciples at the end of the first miracle, 'Who is this that even the wind and the sea obey him?', he is forcing us to draw the inevitable conclusion which the disciples, Mark tells us, were still too stupid, blind and faithless to draw for themselves. That conclusion is that in some undefined sense—but certainly in the most real and powerful sense—Jesus *is* Yahweh himself present on earth."[18]

4. CHANGING WATER INTO WINE AT CANA: JOHN 2:1–11

Theologian David Brown writes of this miracle, "Nothing compels the abandonment of a literal reading, but what can with confidence be asserted is that anyone who makes that meaning primary would have lost the main point of the story, in the marvelous over-abundance of the good and rich life that Christ has come to bring."[19] Brown makes an excellent point. Brown points to all the symbolism in the narrative: the absurd over-provision (120 gallons in modern terms); "the third day"; "my hour…has not yet come"; six jars, that is, one short of the seven of completeness and perfection; the messianic meaning of wine. One might also add that in the Old Testament as well as in later Jewish texts the future messianic days are often depicted as a wedding feast. "As the prophets frequently depict Israel's unfaithfulness to Yahweh as fornication or adultery, so they promise that in the last days he (or his Messiah) shall 'marry' Israel again in an unbroken and eternal covenant. So it is no accident that many stories in the Gospels are about weddings"[20] (see Matt 22:1–10, 11–14; 25:1–12; Luke 12:35–38; 14:7–11). The narrative's primary meaning is theological, and the wedding becomes a symbol of God's kingdom. This is the basic context within which this miracle story is to be understood. The theological meaning is taken forward by Luke Timothy Johnson when he says,

> The prologue [to St. John] begins with a clear allusion to Genesis 1:1, "In the beginning" (John 1:1). Then, for no obvious reason, John dates the next three events in the narrative as "the next day" (1:29), "the next day" (1:35), "the next day" (1:43), and ends here in 2:1 with "on the third day," thus making seven days. Jesus' turning water into wine, then, is a "sign" that the same Word that was at work in the beginning of creation is now, in the body of Jesus, present to transform creation itself into a new and "better" substance.[21]

The huge amount of wine—120 gallons—is also symbolic. A Jewish apocalypse—2 *Baruch* 29:5—that may be contemporary with the Gospel of John predicts that when the last days arrive bringing about the kingdom of God, one grape will produce 120 gallons. It may be that John is alluding to this. This superabundance of wine coming from Jesus is matched with the superabundance of bread coming from him in John 6. In that chapter Jesus speaks of himself as "the bread of life" (John 6:35). Furthermore, Jesus connects himself as the bread of life with the Eucharist when he goes on to say, "Very truly, I tell you, unless you eat the flesh of the Son of Man and drink his blood, you have no life in you. Those who eat my flesh and drink my blood have eternal life, and I will raise them up on the last day; for my flesh is true food and my blood is true drink. Those who eat my flesh and drink my blood abide in me, and I in them" (John 6:53–56). This leads Jeffrey John to comment as follows: "In the Cana story the connection is only allusive, but given the parallelism between the two miracles, in particular the supernatural abundance of bread and wine, and the clear connections with the 'messianic banquet,' it is hard to deny that a Eucharistic reference is present at Cana too. Both miracles were interpreted in a Eucharistic sense in Christian art and theological writing from the second century onwards."[22]

5. FEEDING THE MULTITUDE: MARK 6:30–44; 8:1–9

Taking Mark as the earliest of the Gospels, upon which both Matthew and Luke were dependent, the miracles about feeding the multitudes occur in Mark 6:30–44 (Matt 14:13–21; Luke 9:12–17) and Mark 8:1–9 (Matt 15:32–38). Jeffrey John is particularly helpful here. "Far from seeing [feeding the multitudes] as a straightforward demonstration of divine power or as a moral lesson about caring and sharing...we have to appreciate that, whatever history may lie behind it, this story in its present form is a literary creation with the theological purpose."[23] Having laid down this interpretative principle he goes on to draw it out:

> Perhaps its most obvious theological aim is to tell us that Jesus is a new Moses. Even a modern reader with a sketchy knowledge of the Old Testament is likely to remember that Moses had done something similar with the manna in the desert, and closer examination reveals more detailed points of comparison. Like Moses, Jesus crosses the water into the desert, sits the people down in companies and feeds them with miraculous bread from heaven in such abundance that there are basketfuls leftover. Much less obviously, because the relevant Old Testament story is less well known, Jesus' actions also recall Elisha. Some of the details of the story are clearly taken from an incident in 2 Kings 4 when Elisha takes an army of men into the desert and feeds them miraculously with a few loaves. Taking Elisha and Moses together, the story seems to be telling us in an allusive way that in recapitulating what Moses did Jesus fulfills the Law, and in recapitulating Elisha he fulfills the Prophets.[24]

The Elisha story is not well-known and so we will present the passage from 2 Kings 4 here: "A man came from Baal-shalishah, bringing food from the first fruits to the man of God: twenty loaves of barley and fresh ears of grain in his sack. Elisha said, 'Give it to the people and let them eat.' But his servant said, 'How can I set this before a hundred people?'

So he repeated, 'Give it to the people and let them eat, for thus says the LORD, "They shall eat and have some left."' He set it before them, they ate, and had some left, according to the word of the LORD" (vv. 42–44).

Mark 6:34 reads, "As [Jesus] went ashore, he saw a great crowd; and he had compassion for them, because they were like sheep without a shepherd; and he began to teach them many things." The simile "like sheep without a shepherd" is straightforwardly intelligible. However, it becomes even more theologically intelligible when we recognize an allusion to Numbers 27:17. The context is the appointment of a successor to Moses, the appointment of Joshua. The text reads, "Who shall go out before them and come in before them, who shall lead them out and bring them in, so that the congregation of the LORD may not be like sheep without a shepherd." If St. Mark has this Numbers text in mind, and accepting that in Greek "Joshua" and "Jesus" are the same name, he may well have seen this text as applying to Jesus. Thus,

> Jesus not only "fulfills" Moses and Elijah and Joshua but also supersedes them. No less than in the sea-miracles, to which the two feeding miracles in Mark are each closely tied, Jesus acts here in the power and person of God himself. In Ezekiel God says, "I myself will search for my sheep and rescue them....I will feed them with good pasture..." (Ezekiel 34:11–16). In Isaiah it is Yahweh who will prepare the feast for all peoples when death is swallowed up forever (Isaiah 25:6–8). Or one may also see Jesus here, as in the miracle of the wedding at Cana, in the role of the eternal Wisdom of God, offering herself to human beings in an overflowing banquet of bread and wine (Proverbs 9:1–5; Ecclesiasticus 15:3).[25]

Mark 8:19–20 has Jesus say the following: "'When I broke the five loaves for the five thousand, how many baskets full of broken pieces did you collect?' They said to him, 'Twelve.' 'And the seven for the four thousand, how many baskets full of broken pieces did you collect?' And they said to him, 'Seven.'" The commentary of Jeffrey John is both very illuminating and singularly persuasive:

> Clearly the numbers are symbolic, intended to point us towards interpreting the first miracle as a feeding for Jews, and the second as a feeding for Gentiles. The number five may be regarded as a "Jewish" number because of its relation to the Pentateuch, the five books of the Law; the number four may recall the four winds, the four corners of the earth or the four "beasts" in Daniel (the latter stand for the four Gentile empires that had overrun Israel). The number twelve recalls the twelve tribes, while the number seven had Gentile connotations, seventy being the conventional number of the Gentile nations. Alternatively, seven may simply represent "fullness" here, as it does in many scriptural texts. This interpretation in terms of Jew and Gentile is strengthened by the fact that the first miracle takes place in a Jewish area near the sea of Galilee, the second in the Decapolis, a predominantly Gentile area; and two different Greek words for "basket" used in the two miracles are also said to derive from the two different cultures. The two stories, then, must have been understood by Mark and Matthew as a sort of prefiguring of the two-stage preaching of the gospel: "to the Jew first, then to the Greek" in Paul's phrase. Possibly the second miracle was omitted by Luke and John simply

> because, in the time and context of their writing, the mission to the Gentiles was an undisputed fact, and is expressed by them and many other, less allusive ways. The primary symbolic meaning of the bread is the Word of God, the message of salvation, which was to include Gentiles as well as Jews.[26]

Within the canon of Scripture, the feeding miracles find echoes in the Old Testament. Mark 6:5 and 8:4 refer to a "desert place." This recalls God feeding the people of Israel in the wilderness (Exod 16:4–36; Num 11:7–9; Deut 8:3, 16; Pss 78; 105:40). Jesus satisfies the crowd following him just as God satisfied the hunger of the Israelites of old. Mark 6:34 tells us that Jesus was moved to pity for the crowd because "they were like sheep without a shepherd." In Numbers 27:16–17, Moses says to God, "Let the LORD, the God of the spirits of all flesh, appoint someone over the congregation…who shall lead them out and bring them in, so that the congregation of the LORD may not be like sheep without a shepherd." The feeding of the multitude in Mark replicates in a sense God's feeding and leading the Israelites. What God had done long ago Jesus is doing now. The emphasis is less on the "miraculous" events taking place, and much more on its christological significance pointing to who Jesus is.

Finally, we may say of this feeding narrative that it has to do with the Eucharist. In Mark 6:41 we find the four classic Eucharistic verbs—Jesus *taking* bread, *blessing* it, *breaking* it, and *giving* it. "At least, it is clear to us that in the feeding stories, even in St. Mark's version, we do not have simple straightforward historical accounts of 'what happened,' but elaborately theological interpretations which have turned the historical facts into profound parables of the significance of the person of Christ and of the Eucharist in his church."[27]

6. THE RAISING OF THE WIDOW'S SON AT NAIN: LUKE 7:11–17

This story found only in the Gospel of St. Luke is patterned after Elijah's raising of the widow's son at Zarephath in 1 Kings 17:8–24. A quick comparison of both stories will point out the commonalities, especially the fact that the townspeople of Nain regard Jesus as "a great *prophet*" like Elijah, and both Elijah and Jesus, we are told, "gave him to his mother," identical words in the Septuagint and in Luke. St. Luke casts Jesus as fulfilling the role of the prophet Elijah. Jeffrey John provides a fine summary:

> Several stories about Jesus that occur only in Luke directly recall stories about Elijah: for example, the disciples' desire to call down fire on their enemies (Luke 9:54); and the story of the disciple who wishes to say goodbye to his family (Luke 9:61–62). Only in Luke's gospel does Jesus at the start of his ministry deliberately compare himself to Elijah and Elisha, both of whom had a ministry to Gentiles; he specifically recalls the raising of the widow's son at Zarephath (Luke 4:25–26). But as well as being attracted by Elijah as a forerunner of the Gentile mission, Luke was clearly strongly influenced as well by the tradition that having been taken up into heaven, Elijah sent down his spirit on Elisha, who continued his work and repeated some of his miracles. In the same way, it is only in Luke–Acts that Jesus ascends, and then sends down his Spirit upon the disciples, who are thus empowered to do works similar to his own."[28]

Perhaps needless to point out, however, the major difference between Elijah and Jesus is that Elijah calls on God to heal the widow's son, but Jesus brings the boy to life through his own word, "Young man, I say to you, rise!" (Luke 7:14).

7. THE RAISING OF LAZARUS: JOHN 11:38–44

The raising of Lazarus, unique to John's Gospel, is the seventh sign in the Book of Signs in this Gospel. In Luke's Gospel Lazarus is a fictional character in the parable of the rich man with the beggar at his gate (Luke 16:19–31). Jeffrey John comments, "The punchline of Luke's parable is in Abraham's reply: 'I tell you, they will not believe even if one should rise from the dead.' It is hard to avoid the conclusion that John's Gospel, with its typically dark irony, has made Lazarus a real person, and made Luke's punchline come true. Lazarus does indeed come back from the dead; but so far from this causing others to believe, it becomes the main reason why Jesus himself is put to death."[29]

To access the full theological significance of the sign of Lazarus in John it is necessary to turn to John 5:25–29:

> Very truly, I tell you, the hour is coming, and is now here, when the dead will hear the voice of the Son of God, and those who hear will live. For just as the Father has life in himself, so he has granted the Son also to have life in himself; and he has given him authority to execute judgment, because he is the Son of Man. Do not be astonished at this; for the hour is coming when all who are in their graves will hear his voice and will come out—those who have done good, to the resurrection of life,

> and those who have done evil, to the resurrection of condemnation.

The story of Lazarus is a dramatization of those words. "Lazarus, the one Jesus loves, is…the representative of all those whom Jesus loves, namely the Christians. Just as Jesus gives life to his beloved Lazarus, so he will give life to his beloved Christians."[30] "Lazarus, in other words, stands for us."[31]

CONCLUSION

One can look at the nature miracles performed by Jesus in at least two ways. First, one might read them as an exact historical account of what Jesus did. Second, one might read them in a more symbolical mode, seeing in them invitations not only to christological insight but also to discipleship. This chapter has approached the nature miracles emphasizing the second way of reading. This second way of reading the nature miracles, as primarily symbolical-christological, gathers strength when one looks at some of the contributions of contemporary theologians writing about the miraculous. That will be the contribution of a later chapter. In the meantime, attention will be given to the meaning of the miraculous throughout the Christian tradition: the patristic period, the medieval period, and the Enlightenment.

CHAPTER 5

PATRISTIC AND MEDIEVAL MIRACLES

In the ancient or medieval world the statement "the world is full of miracles" would not have meant "the constant infraction of the course of this world," principally because the notion of the law of nature was not used in opposition to the nature of creation by God; it would have meant "everything created is a wonder issuing from the hand of God."

Benedicta Ward[1]

Very little direct discussion of miracles took place from the time of Augustine to that of Thomas Aquinas. No treatise *De Miraculis* (Concerning Miracles) survives in which the concept of the miraculous is discussed and related to other kinds of reality.

Benedicta Ward[2]

INTRODUCTION

The Bible contains a variety of words for which the English word *miracle* is the usual translation. Restricting the vocabulary to the New Testament one notices that "one of the striking facts about the vocabulary of 'miracle' in the New Testament is the extreme rarity of any word that...corresponds to the word 'miracle'; for, broadly speaking, the words most used are not *thaumasion* ('marvel'), but *dunamis* ('power') and *semeion* ('sign')."[3] Now, of course, a developing theology of the miraculous cannot rest on points of vocabulary alone, but, in conjunction with the first opening citation from the historian of medieval theology Sister Benedicta Ward, we may be alerted to at least the possibility that dictionary definitions of *miracle* may owe more to the Enlightenment and its rationalist presuppositions than to a fair reading of the Christian tradition.

MIRACLES IN THE PATRISTIC PERIOD

In ancient society "stories about miracle workers were common; and the proliferation of magical papyri, amulets, tablets of various materials, and magical bowls, point to the commonplace character of such practices."[4] In early Christian literature, miracles were performed for different purposes. One purpose might be to establish the divine authority of a preacher, as in the *Acts of John* 39. Another purpose is to support the witness of the martyr, and an example of this is provided in the *Acts of Paul*, in which Thecla, fellow worker of St. Paul, is delivered miraculously from death in the arena. Again, miracle working can take on the form of a competition, such as that described between St. Peter and Simon Magus in the *Acts of Peter*. Geoffrey Lampe, the patristic theologian, points out that "all this belongs essentially to the realm of popular fiction."[5] Having readily admitted this with Lampe, however, it goes without saying that patristic authors, both before and after Emperor Constantine and the edict of Milan that provided toleration for Christianity, accepted the historicity of the gospel miracles.

The earliest Christian apologist was Quadratus, living and writing in the early second century. About the year 124, Quadratus wrote an apology for the Christian faith, which he addressed to the Roman emperor Hadrian. This is now lost, but a single fragment survives in Eusebius's *Ecclesiastical History*.[6] Quadratus defends the historicity of Jesus's miracles in this fashion: that some of the people who had been healed by Jesus lived for a considerable period of time after his departure and that some of them survived "even to our own day." Unfortunately, the fragment of Quadratus does not provide us with any detailed information about such persons, and he himself claims no personal knowledge of them. And so, while in principle his argument might have a degree of persuasiveness about it, as time passes "in the next generation it would be altogether too late to carry on the argument in this fashion."[7] Later Christian thinkers developed a different line. They argued that, if the earliest disciples of Jesus had fabricated these miracle stories, what possible inducement could there have been for them to incur hardships, suffering, and even death? Geoffrey Lampe puts it well:

> Why should they actually deny and forsake Jesus during his earthly life, only to deify him after he had died a shameful death? Why, after his death, should they incur death themselves, just in order to provide him with a false posthumous reputation? They might have been able to bamboozle peasants in their own country, but they could not have

> hoped, on this basis, to evangelize the whole world from Persia to Britain. Such a conspiracy would have had to be most complicated, involving agreement between all the disciples to pre-fabricate the same tale.[8]

What about sorcery? Critics of early Christianity accused Jesus of being a sorcerer. For example, Celsus seems to have acknowledged Christ's miracles as historical events, but at the same time he believed that Christ had acquired these magical powers in Egypt.[9] Origen's reply is to appeal to the consistent moral teaching and record of the Gospels: "Why, then, asks Origen, did Christ bother about ethical teaching? What has that to do with the magician? (1.38). He who reformed men morally cannot have been a sorcerer (1.68)."[10]

This emphasis on the importance of the moral dimension over the purely miraculous, as it were, continues in the tradition. One example that comes to mind is Tertullian of Carthage. He argued that when Jesus healed the man born blind, this healing was symbolic of Jesus's enlightenment of Judaism. Yet, he also insists that the healing did take place.[11] "Symbolic allegorism existed in harmony with a general acceptance of the *thaumata* (wondrous deeds) of Jesus."[12] A symbolic interpretation of miracle went together with an acceptance of historicity.

In the same way, later Christian authors undoubtedly accepted and reaffirmed the historicity of the gospel miracles. At the same time, however, they pointed out the superiority of the moral argument. Taking John Chrysostom as his exemplar, patristic scholar and theologian Maurice Wiles illustrates this point as follows:

> John Chrysostom argues that the spiritual side of the redeemed Christian is a better sign than the

> physical healing of the blind man. The latter is open to suspicion (even if unjustifiable suspicion in the case of the Christian miracles) and may (as in the case of Simon Magus) give rise to no more than a desire to get the same power for oneself. It is a better sign to be ready to die for one's faith than to be able to raise the dead; to despise money as grass than to be able to turn grass into money.[13]

At the same time, the same John Chrysostom recognizes the historicity of the gospel miracles.[14] John also tackles the question why there are so few miracles in his time. He explains this by proposing that miracles were necessary when the nascent Christian church was expanding in missionary outreach throughout the Roman Empire. They became much less necessary once the church was well established.[15]

In the literature surrounding the desert fathers there are all kinds of miracles, not in the reflections of the monks themselves so much, but in the comments of visitors and outsiders.[16] The monks themselves were down-to-earth individuals, aware of their sinfulness and of their need to repent, constantly striving against the temptation to pride. Benedicta Ward, established authority on desert monasticism, writes, "Some stories about the monks gained miraculous overtones in the retelling by outsiders of events which had been to the monastic participants part of the coincidences of a life of prayer. The well-known story of a young monk who was told by an elder to plant a dead stick and continually water it, was told among the monks as an outstanding example of obedience and nothing more; but when repeated by an outsider there was the addition that the stick miraculously flowered."[17] The monks were in the desert in order to find their way to God, perhaps especially through their coping with suffering in those challenging surroundings, and they were not particularly interested in miraculous phenomena that might seem to distract from their moral and spiritual project.

If we turn to the apocryphal *Acts—Acts of John, Acts of Paul, Acts of Peter*—the miraculous element tends to become more spectacular. Some argue that the motive for this spectacular dimension is to attract and to convert people to Christian faith. While there seems to be something in that, perhaps especially respective of illiterate and uneducated persons, there also appears to be something else at work, namely, entertainment. One scholar writes, "In all of this we should note that miracle stories also functioned to entertain. This is clear in the canonical Acts of the Apostles (see Acts 28), as it is in the apocryphal acts where stories of talking dogs, resurrected fish and expelled bed bugs are there to amuse as well as to make theological points."[18]

St. Augustine

"For Augustine, and his hearers and readers, the central miracle was redemption; contemporary miracles were seen in relation to the life of conversion of the redeemed. They were evidences of grace abounding, ways of recognizing and entering into the central miracle of Christ's redeeming work."[19] This is true, of course, of the whole patristic period and not simply of St. Augustine himself. Creation was miraculous as the work of God, and re-creation was even more miraculous because of the incarnation and the redemptive work of the Lord. This is the foundation principle from which Augustine views miracles. At the same time, "Slowly but surely Augustine identifies himself with the devotions of his people. He never despises their longing for supernatural signs of divine presence."[20] This statement by Henry Chadwick directs us to appreciate Augustine's approach to the miraculous. He was not particularly taken up with the miraculous as such, but he recognized it as part and parcel of the devotional life of Christians.

In Augustine's treatise of 390, *On True Religion,* we read, "If we look for a cause of all and wonder now, we should contemplate nature" (16.34), and in his *Tract on the Gospel of St. John,* "The daily miracles of creation are as great as those of the incarnate Lord" (9.1). These reflections provide us with Augustine's deeply held personal point of view on the miraculous. Yet, he not only acknowledges the place of miracles in the devotional life of Christians generally but also recognizes their role in evangelization.

Benedicta Ward helpfully reminds us of the context in which Augustine was writing: "The barbarian invasions caused a new need for teaching and preaching and wonders were very often the best contact with the pagans. They were a converting medium and also a reassurance to Christians under threat."[21] In his *The City of God,* Augustine was attempting to refute the pagan accusation that it was Christianity that caused the fall of Rome to the barbarians. The key text is *The City of God* 22.8–9.[22] Immediately Augustine recognizes the recording of miracles in the Scriptures, most especially the resurrection of Christ. At the same time, miracles have to do with faith. "[Miracles] have become known in order to promote faith; they have become more widely known through the faith which they promoted. The accounts are read among the nations, so that the people may believe; but they would never have been read, had they not been believed" (22.8). Augustine goes on to describe a number of miracles: a blind man of Milan whose sight was restored through the relics of the martyrs Gervasius and Protasius; the healing of a friend, Innocentius, who had undergone a number of surgeries but was finally healed through prayer; and a number of healings through the relics of martyrs or at shrines. Augustine is careful to point out that miracles connected with martyrs' shrines are "the work of God, with the co-operation of the martyrs or in response to their prayers" (22.10). He wishes to avoid at all costs the suggestion that such Christian miracles are on the same level as accounts of the miraculous supposedly brought about by pagan deities. But, before he enters into these lengthy accounts of miracles, he briefly makes this very important comment: "Even now miracles are being performed in Christ's name either by his sacrament, or by the prayers or the memorials of his saints, but they do not enjoy the blaze of publicity which would spread their fame with a glory to equal that of those earlier marvels" (22.8). Notice that before mentioning miracles that come about "by the prayers or the memorials of saints," he speaks of miracles being performed "in Christ's name...by his sacrament." A strong sacramental realism of Christ working through the sacraments appears to have primacy in Augustine's understanding, and, in fact, a number of the miracles that he goes on to relate have to do with the sacrament of baptism. The new or deepening identity of Christians as the Body of Christ through the sacraments at times effects miraculous events.

According to St. Augustine, when God acts in his normal and usual manner, that is called nature. When God acts in an unusual way in order to instruct and teach humankind, that is called a miracle. Here is a passage from the *De Trinitate*:

> It is by the power of God administering the whole spiritual and corporeal universe that on certain days every year the waters of the sea are summoned and poured out as rain on the face of the earth. But once upon a time this happened at the prayer of Elijah, after such a long and unbroken drought that men were dying of famine; at the moment the servant of God made his prayer the weather had shown no signs, such as a damp and cloudy face to the

> sky, of the rain that will soon come; thus when the rainstorm followed so rapidly and in such quantity on the heels of his prayer, the power of God was made manifest to those who were given the benefit of that miracle....When these things happen in the continuous flow and flux of things..., they are called natural; when however, to teach men some lesson, they are pressed forward in some abnormal transformation, they are called the wonderful works of God.[23]

The passage shows us the ordinary working of God in the events of nature, in this case the rain, and also the extraordinary working of God in the miracle associated with Elijah the prophet (see 1 Kgs 18). This way of understanding leads one commentator to say, "With the eyes of faith St. Augustine sees with the same clarity the mark of divine love and power in the gathering of a harvest as in the multiplication of the loaves."[24] Symbolic interpretation of the miraculous goes hand in hand with acceptance of historicity.

Benedicta Ward offers us a most clear summary description of Augustine's approach: "[Miracles] were wonderful acts of God shown as events in this world, not in opposition to nature but as a drawing out of the hidden workings of God within a nature that was all potentially miraculous."[25] For St. Augustine anything in creation could, at least potentially, tell of God. In fact, as Ward goes on to inform us, Augustine considered that there were three levels of wonder/miracle: "wonder provoked by the acts of God visible daily and discerned by wise men as signs of God's goodness; wonder provoked in the ignorant, who did not understand the workings of nature and therefore could be amazed by what to the wise man was not unusual; and wonder provoked by genuine miracles, unusual manifestations of the power of God, not *contra naturam* (against nature) but *praeter* or *supra naturam*."[26] St. Augustine writes, "I call that miraculous which appears wonderful because it is either hard or impossible, beyond hope or ability."[27] For Augustine, whether an event happened in nature or happened miraculously is not especially to the point because, in fact, in both spheres it is the work of God. "Some things happen naturally, others miraculously; God works in whatever is natural and he is not apart from the wonders of nature."[28]

By way of summary these patristic authors, and especially St. Augustine, are more interested in miracles as signs of salvation, of God at work in creation and redemption and so in the church as in a kind of continuum rather than in miracles as manifestations of divine omnipotence.[29] This was to change with the movement away from Platonism as the general philosophical background of Christian theology during the patristic period to Aristotelianism, with its greater emphasis on cause and effect, in the Middle Ages. Aristotelianism represents a more empirical approach to reality. We may see this general movement first in St. Anselm of Canterbury in the twelfth century and then more systematically in St. Thomas Aquinas in the thirteenth century. "The main question was no longer: What is God's purpose in the miracle? Or, how can man best reply to this purpose within the ambit of his devotional life? It rather became: What exactly is the nature of the divine intervention which the miracle involves?"[30]

MIRACLES AND THE MEDIEVAL MIND

Miracles and the Medieval Mind is the title of a magisterial study by Sister Benedicta Ward. Her title not only is concise but contains the nucleus of what she wishes to convey. Ward recognizes that while her book is but "a preliminary approach to one portion of a vast, complex, and unstable mass of material," nonetheless miracle stories or records are an important segue into an understanding of the medieval mind. She points out that while medieval historians have access to all kinds of data in their research (e.g., charters, grants, wills, letters, tracts of various kinds, etc.), miracle stories are seldom used and yet are not less important in reaching into the "medieval mind."[31]

In his treatise *De Conceptu Virginali* (*On the Virginal Conception*), St. Anselm of Canterbury distinguished miracles from natural events and from events that came about as a result of human free will: "So if we consider carefully everything that is done, we see that they happen either by the will of God alone, or by nature according to the power God has given it, or by the will of a creature. Now, those things which are done neither by created nature nor by the will of the creature but by God alone, are miracles: so it seems that there are three ways in which things happen, that is, the miraculous, the natural and the voluntary."[32] Miracles in Anselm's understanding are caused by divine intervention in creation and are not simply to be understood as events that call for human wonder. Benedicta Ward comments, "This shift from the sacramental view of the whole order of creation as miraculous"—largely the patristic perspective—"in which the power of God could be seen as a sign to men in all events, emphasized, from another point of view, the new freedom to examine the natural events; it also intended to limit the events that could properly be called miracles."[33] New ways of doing philosophy were at work, new ways of looking empirically at the world.

As Ward notes, "From the eleventh and twelfth centuries...it seems that thought about miracles underwent some changes. Perhaps 'change' is too strong a word; it was more that the traditional approach to miracles continued and deepened especially in monastic circles, until it emerged as so interior that it could quite easily be divorced from external reality altogether. Meanwhile, a secondary theme, the mechanics of events, always there but rarely emerging, became more prominent until it took over altogether later as science."[34] The key figure here is St. Bernard of Clairvaux. St. Bernard demonstrates an interest in the interior or spiritual view of miracles as well as in miracles as external events. The interior view of miracles had to do with conversion of heart, the performance of good works, and the cultivation of the virtues. For Bernard and for others of his time, "*miracula exteriora* (external and visible miracles) and *miracula interiora* (internal-spiritual and invisible miracles) are both expected with the former in service of the latter. Authentic works of power, whether exterior or interior, are intended to increase sanctity."[35] In this regard the premier exemplar was the Blessed Virgin Mary. "In her, the greatest of miracles took place; God became man, the virgin became a mother, the Word became flesh."[36] The miracle of the incarnation that came about with Mary's consent was unsurpassed as miracle. As a result, the one who kept all these things in her heart (Luke 2:19) exemplified in a perfect degree conversion of heart, good works, and all the virtues. Mary was the mother of monks and so, for example, summoned and encouraged them to similar interior miracles.

The later Middle Ages witnessed a development in respect for Mary. All kinds of "external" miracles were attributed to her, especially at important Marian pilgrimage shrines. Miracles were also associated with physical relics of Mary—her slipper, her hair, droplets of milk from her breast, and so forth. These supposedly physical relics are interesting not least because of the early patristic conviction of Mary's assumption into heaven after her death.[37] "Miracles as interior conversion and exterior cure were held together throughout the Middle Ages, but a new attitude which challenged this understanding was the approach which asked the question 'how' instead of providing the reason 'why' miracles took place: looking at the past mechanics of an event rather than its then-current meaning."[38] Even so, Benedicta Ward is careful to point out that miracles continue to be seen by the eyes of faith, of faithful vision in the presence and action of God, and not simply with one's physical eyes. That was altogether secondary, even when the mechanics of a miracle were being analyzed.

"Between Augustine and Aquinas, there was no major philosophical treatise on miracles."[39] Aquinas makes an important distinction. He distinguishes the "wonder" that flows from someone's ignorance of the causes that are at work in nature from the "wonder" that is genuinely and inherently wonderful "because it truly has no natural cause."[40] If someone has no understanding of science at all, then he may think of something as in our terms "miraculous" that may be in fact quite easily explainable in scientific terms. He also acknowledges, however, that there are such events that cannot be explained in scientific terms.[41] Aquinas's analytic methodology is far more interested than Augustine in identifying causes. This is probably because, under the influence of Aristotle, "he has a greater interest in the way the natural world works, and because he was more confident about our discovering and reliably identifying such causal powers and, relatedly, because the concept of causal power has more widely useful explanatory work to do in Aquinas's philosophizing."[42] Thus, Aquinas can write: "It is...certain that divine power can sometimes produce an effect, without prejudice to its providence, apart from the order implanted in natural things by God. In fact, he does this at times to manifest power. For it can be manifested in no better way, that the whole of nature is subject to the divine will, than by the fact that sometimes he does something outside the order of nature. Indeed, this makes it evident that the order of things has proceeded from him, not by natural necessity, but by free will."[43] He considers that the teaching of Jesus Christ and his being God are confirmed by the miracles attributed to him in the Gospels. The miracles of the Gospels could occur only through the power of God. If Jesus worked such miracles, then these point to his divinity.[44] This was a powerful apologetic point for St. Thomas over against Islam. Aquinas thought that Muhammad's failure to give miraculous signs was a clear indication of Islam's inferiority to Christianity, as in his *Summa Contra Gentiles* 1.6. In fact, there is a Surah in the *Qur'an* that explicitly and intentionally distances Muhammad from miracles. "Non-believers say 'Unless he works a miracle, we will not believe.' Tell them you are commissioned to be a preacher only, not a miracle-worker."[45]

In the Middle Ages miracle stories attached themselves to the Eucharist. Benedicta Ward tells us that three kinds of miracles were connected with the Eucharist: what came to be known as "the miracle of the Mass"; visions and miracles that illustrated the Mass; miracles that demonstrated the power of the Mass in particular situations. Primarily because of the vigorous discussion that arose concerning eucharistic realism in the ninth century around the monks of Corbie, Paschasius Radbertus and Ratramnus, attention began to be focused on the eucharistic host as itself miraculous. Bread and wine had been changed into the same body that Jesus received from the Blessed Virgin Mary at his conception. In the eleventh and twelfth centuries, as a result of this concentration on the host, visions of the Christ child were seen in the host. This contrasts with earlier generations' concern with the church as the body of Christ. "It is not so much the 'body of Christ which is the church' as 'the body of Christ which is the host', and the host itself had been changed by a miracle."[46] The general patristic theological point of view was that Christ had three bodies and these three were one: the body taken from the Blessed Virgin Mary and now gloriously transformed through the resurrection, the eucharistic body, and the ecclesial body. Now, with the onset of debates about the precise meaning of the eucharistic body/the eucharistic presence of Christ, the balance of the patristic point of view was largely lost. The emphasis was now on the eucharistic body of Christ.[47]

The second category of eucharistic miracles focused on the Christ child appearing in the host, and sometimes the figure of the crucified Christ appearing in the host, with his blood flowing into the chalice during the celebration of Mass. Ward remarks that there was a flood of such stories, all pointing to the "miraculous" change that had occurred during the liturgical celebration.

The third category of eucharistic miracles is slightly different. "In these the consecrated elements themselves were regarded as a permanent focus of power, just as a relic was held to be....The host was placed along with the relics of saints in altars at their consecration....The host was a relic among relics, dignified only because it was the relic of Christ."[48] The Fourth Lateran Council in 1215 forbade the host being taken out of the church, pointing to the belief that the host was an object of immense power that could be used for practical purposes.

The modern understanding of miracle as a direct intervention of God in the normal course of events is "a narrow and modern concept, which had little meaning before the sixteenth century at the earliest."[49] Benedicta Ward very clearly outlines a rather different worldview, the worldview of the Middle Ages:

> The world was the antechamber of heaven, and [Gregory the Great] made sure that his readers

> understood that they had friends at court who would intercede for them in their needs and difficulties. This familiarity with the saints and the increasing desire to be in physical, practical contact with them by visiting the place where their bodies lay created the great shrines and pilgrimage routes of the Middle Ages. These remained, in however distant and confused a way, an image of men within the household of faith, exiles continually returning to their home country of heaven. In this context, the miracles of the saints were simply the ordinary life of heaven made manifest in earthly affairs, chinks in the barriers between heaven and earth, a situation in which not to have miracles was a cause of surprise, terror, and dismay.[50]

The miracles in this context have become powerful and persuasive sacraments of the communion of saints.

CONCLUSION

Toward the end of her essay "Monks and Miracles," Benedicta Ward has a fine paragraph that opens on to a later Enlightenment attitude to the phenomenon. She refuses an either-or approach, advocating a both-and approach:

> Two understandings of miracles, then, seem to be intertwined in all Christian consideration of the miraculous; miracles as marvels and miracles as signs. It seems that it was the idea of miracles presented as wonders that provoked the challenging question "How can that happen?' while the concept of miracle as sign continued to center on the

> interior investigation of "Why did this happen? What is its meaning for me?" To pose the question "'How?" to any event need not exclude the older question, "Why?" There is no reason why the two approaches to miracles should not be equally useful. One way of thinking can increase wonder rather than diminish it while the other leads into the fundamental question for mankind in relation to God.[51]

As with so much of her careful historical-theological research, Benedicta Ward has enabled us to appreciate a very holistic approach to miracle during the patristic and medieval periods. That holistic approach was to begin to break down with the onset of the development in European thought that has come to be known as the Enlightenment, and so it is to the Enlightenment that we must now turn our attention.

CHAPTER 6

THE ENLIGHTENMENT AND MIRACLES

> The essential point about mid-eighteenth-century Britain is that a range of ideas and opinions on the miraculous and the wondrous, the ordinary and the extraordinary, existed.
>
> Jane Shaw[1]

> The Enlightenment arguments specifically against the apologists' use of miracle reports are due mainly to Hume.
>
> Joseph Houston[2]

The term *Enlightenment* is applied to the movement of ideas that characterized much of eighteenth-century Europe, a movement that distrusted authority and tradition when it came to intellectual inquiry. Essentially, Enlightenment thinkers were committed to the principle that truth could be attained only through reason, observation, and experiment.

In this new era, "the role of reason was magnified, that of revelation was depressed. The Scriptures were subjected to intensive and often to unsympathetic scrutiny. Miracles were challenged. Prophecy was reassessed. Christian thought faced a threat which might have stripped it of all its uniqueness and its authority."[3] From the point of view of this book on miracles, the most important critical thinker when it came to the miraculous was the Scottish philosopher David Hume (1711–76). In his 1748 book *Of Miracles,* Hume adopted a skeptical attitude toward miracles, but if we are to appreciate his contribution to the discussion, we must begin a little earlier than the eighteenth century.

SEVENTEENTH-CENTURY ENGLAND

A belief in miracles has been a constant feature of Catholicism. In the years following the sixteenth-century Reformation, Protestantism distanced itself from postbiblical miracles, a position often referred to as "cessationism." Yet, as has been well established by church historian Jane Shaw, there were three major attitudes within Protestantism to miracles in seventeenth-century England: the commonplace idea that miracles had ceased to occur after the end of the biblical period (cessationism); the development among some independent churches and radical Protestant sects that claimed healing and miracles; and, finally, a middle path maintaining that miracles, while plausible, had to be carefully investigated.

Miracles associated with holy places and objects were commonplace in medieval England, two of the most important centers being the shrine of St. Thomas Beckett in Canterbury and that of Our Lady of Walsingham in Norfolk. Through the Reformation the idea became widespread that miracles had ceased by the end of biblical times, and many of these later miracles were viewed with suspicion. "Signs and wonders were to be discarded for the promises made by God in his Word."[4] Scripture, and often Scripture alone, was now all-important, and no intermediary, including saints and holy places and places of pilgrimage, was needed for the individual's relationship with God. Especially after the dissolution of the monasteries by King Henry VIII in the 1530s, many of these "miracle-centers" simply ceased to exist, and "the medieval past was rewritten by the Protestant Reformation propagandists to discredit Catholicism."[5] While the Protestant Reformation discounted postbiblical miracles, the Catholic Reformation, or Counter-Reformation, continued to support them, and both sides argued their positions in polemical literature. It is important to emphasize that the Protestant Reformers did not deny the reality of miracles in the Bible, nor did they support a skeptical questioning of them. It was the miracles of the postbiblical period to which they were greatly opposed. No intermediary of any kind was needed between God and the devout believer.

Now we come to the claim to work miracles on the part of some independent churches and radical Protestant sects, what might be called "folk religion" or the experienced religiosity of the populace at large. Jane Shaw writes, "The mid-seventeenth century witnessed not only the revival of an intra-Protestant debate about whether miracles had ceased or not, based on the claims of certain groups to be able to work them and to have experienced them in their own age, but also the beginnings of an interaction between those claims and the new practices and theories that were emerging, aimed at investigating, understanding and explaining the natural world—that is, what historians used to call the 'Scientific Revolution.'"[6] The Quakers were one of these Protestant groups that believed in healing, and their founder

George Fox (1624–91) did not hesitate to call these healings miracles. These miraculous cures were most often effected by the laying on of hands or speaking some quiet words over the sick person, both arguably sound biblical gestures. Nevertheless, the Quakers found themselves often ridiculed in this respect. Whether or not and to what extent there was a "Scientific Revolution" is a matter for the historians to decide. What is not in dispute, however, is the development of an empirically based methodology that sought natural explanations for these supposedly miraculous phenomena, and, of course, as such methodologies became well known and widespread, the quest for natural explanations began to look also at the miracles of the biblical period. "Or to put it another way: the 'Enlightenment' had arrived."[7]

Toward the end of the seventeenth century and as a result of the developing, empirical methodologies of the Enlightenment, what may be called a new development in the attitude to miracles occurred. Faced with a certain "enthusiasm" about miracles from such groups as the Quakers and with the emerging empirical methodologies, Anglican (and other) theologians in England had to find a middle way. That middle path was between enthusiasm and atheism (though that is probably at this time too strong a term), those who happily believed in miracles and, indeed, experienced them and those who were skeptical not only of the alleged contemporary experiences but also of the biblical miracles. It was virtually inevitable that skepticism about contemporary cures would lead to skepticism about the cures brought about by Jesus and others in the New Testament. That leads Jane Shaw to say, "Those Protestants who had declared the cessation of miracles, while not questioning God's ability to work miracles, nevertheless provided the foundation for a key Enlightenment question: did God work miracles at all?...This caused problems for those 'middle way' Anglicans and reasonable dissenters who wished to balance reason and revelation, perceiving that such a balance was essential to a stable religious situation."[8] As the Enlightenment developed during the eighteenth century, "this middle way was to take," in Shaw's words, "something of an intellectual battering." The intellectual battering is demonstrated in the plethora of books and pamphlets on the subject of miracles during the first half of the eighteenth century so that one commentator writes, "At its height—around the 1720s—the debate had received enormous attention; so much so that almost every English theologian, philosopher, or even simply man of letters of the period made some contribution to it."[9]

By the middle of the eighteenth century a split had taken place between what Jane Shaw calls "lived religion," that is, the experienced religiosity of the ordinary people, and intellectual debate. John Wesley (1703–91), the founder of the Methodist movement, clearly believed in miraculous healings, some of which he mentions in his *Journal*. Just two years before David Hume published his essay on miracles, John Wesley wrote in a letter,

> And I acknowledge that I have seen with my eyes and heard with my ears several things, which, to the best of my judgment, cannot be accounted for by the ordinary course of natural causes, and which I therefore believe to be ascribed to the extraordinary interposition of God. If any man choose to study these miracles, I reclaim not. I have diligently inquired into the facts. I have weighed the preceding and following circumstances. I have strove to account for them in a natural way. I could not without doing violence to my own reason....I must observe that the truth of these facts is supposed by the same kind of proof as that of all other facts is

> wont to be—namely, the testimony of competent witnesses; and that the testimony here is in as high a degree as any reasonable man can desire. Those witnesses were many in number: they could not be deceived themselves; for the facts in question they saw with their own eyes and heard with their own ears, nor is it credible that so many of them would combine together with a view of deceiving others.[10]

In many ways, Wesley represents the "lived religion" of ordinary, devout people. At the same time, one can see in the words of this letter the effects of the new Enlightenment methodology. Wesley himself weighs evidence carefully and makes the point of relying on the testimony of witnesses. If Wesley exemplifies the experiential/lived religion side of the split in the mid-eighteenth century, undoubtedly the one who contributed most to the intellectual debate side of the split and had more influence than any other was Wesley's contemporary, David Hume.

DAVID HUME (1711–76)

A native of Edinburgh, Scotland, David Hume wanted to be a philosopher from an early age. He lived in France from 1734 to 1737, and this is where he worked out the principles of his three-volume work, the *Treatise of Human Nature* (1739–40). Some years later in 1748 he published his *Philosophical Essays Concerning Human Understanding*, and this is the volume in which may be found his famous "Essay on Miracles." This essay on miracles has received "more critical attention than anything else Hume wrote on religion. Its particular merits may not justify this but its importance in his whole critique of religion within the limits of reason alone can scarcely be overestimated."[11]

"A wise man proportions his belief to the evidence," says Hume.[12] Hume relies primarily on the experience afforded by the senses, perhaps what we might call "commonsense experience." Basically, Hume is right. If we come across what seems to be an outlandish account of an event or happening, our immediate and intelligent response is one of qualified skepticism. We want to regard the evidence. This is true not only of egregiously strange events but also of simple daily observation. We rely on our ordinary experience as we reach toward the truth. Hume writes, "Should a traveler, returning from a far country, bring us an account of men, wholly different from any with whom we were ever acquainted; men, who were entirely invested of avarice, ambition or revenge; who knew no pleasure but friendship, generosity, and public spirit; we should immediately, from these circumstances, detect the falsehood, and prove him a liar, with the same certainty as if he had stuffed his narration with stories of centaurs and dragons, miracles and prodigies."[13] That kind of account of human beings does not square with what we know of ordinary people. Human nature being what it is, people are simply not as virtuous as that. So, we are skeptical of the account. Weighing evidence is the normal way human beings proceed in reaching toward truth.

At the same time, there is a necessary reliance on the testimony of other trustworthy people. Hume's essay as such does not set out to show that miracles are logically impossible. Rather, Hume is arguing against the unquestioned acceptance of superstition. "That no testimony is sufficient to establish a miracle, unless the testimony be of such a kind, that its falsehood would be more miraculous than the fact which it endeavors to establish; and even in that case there is a mutual destruction of arguments, and the superior only gives us an assurance suitable to take place to that degree of force, which remains, after deducting the inferior."[14] The Hume scholar John Gaskin summarizes the point well: "Hume's argument tells me that if *I* have seen a miracle I should not expect any reasonable or wise man to believe my report....Hume is simply warning that incredulity is what I should expect. His argument refers explicitly and totally to the credibility of reports of miracles not to the possibility of actually experiencing one take place."[15]

Although Hume targets reports of others concerning miracles, reports that he generally regards as incredulous, his basic attitude to miracles as such is skeptical. Hume offers three examples of three well-substantiated miracles, all based on the testimony of trustworthy people at various times and places. The first one has to do with the Roman emperor Vespasian whom the Roman historian Tacitus reported as having healed a blind man by means of his spittle. The second tells of a miracle that took place in Saragossa in which a man's leg grew from its stump after holy oil had been rubbed on it. This miraculous report comes from Cardinal de Retz (1614–79), who had been archbishop of Paris, and on the surface was presumed by many to be reliable. Since this was closer to Hume's time than Emperor Vespasian, and closeness in time was a crucial factor for Hume, it is worth citing at some length.

> When [Cardinal de Retz] fled into Spain to avoid the persecution of his enemies, he passed through Saragossa, the capital of Aragon, where he was shown in the Cathedral a man who had served seven years as a doorkeeper, and was well known to everybody in town that had ever paid his devotions at that church. He had been seen for so long a time wanting a leg, but recovered that by the rubbing of holy oil upon the stump; and the Cardinal assures us that he saw

> him with two legs. This miracle was vouched by all the canons of the church; and the whole company in town were appealed to for confirmation of the fact; whom the Cardinal found, by their zealous devotion, to be thorough believers of the miracle.[16]

The third example has to do with the many well-attested miracles performed in Paris at the tomb of a saintly Jansenist priest, Abbé Paris. Rather than accept the veracity of such miracles that clearly violate laws of nature, even the two that were closer in time to Hume and so not forfeit to the exaggerations of antiquity, we should be skeptical and account for these stories "by the known and natural principles of credulity and delusion."[17]

Miracles do not occur, and they did not occur—not Hume's own words, but essentially his viewpoint. His approach to the miraculous is essentially negative. That is why John Gaskin goes on to comment as follows: "When Hume lists the factors which put the veracity of an historical report in question, the effect of his argument is to include among them the probability of the event reported.…Disbelief, when the report is suspect and what is reported is grossly improbable, is both normal and rational, and Hume's argument does little more than codify this response."[18] The position of David Hume on miracles was enormously influential, either from his immediate philosophical influence or from the fast-growing skepticism that was consequent upon the Enlightenment. In many ways Hume's position is the regnant philosophical position today.

CONCLUSION

It is incontestable that the Enlightenment and thinkers in its wake tended to view the world of nature and the world of grace as not only distinguishable but entirely separable, something that the medieval world held together and did not separate. This was the worldview "in which the relationship between the supernatural, understood as the divine agency in grace, and the natural or the order of creation were driven apart. If the laws of nature no longer reflected a participation in the divine act of being and the action of God that is concurrent with creaturely agency, then miracles could be understood as a violation of what God or nature constituted as the order of creation."[19] Of course, not every Christian thinker accepted this separation of the two orders. To take but one example, Friedrich Schleiermacher (1768–1834) attempted in his comprehensive theological worldview to maintain a strong continuity between the natural order/creation and the supernatural order/grace. In his *On Religion: Speeches to Its Cultured Despisers*, he writes, "Every finite thing, however, is a sign of the Infinite....Miracle is simply the religious name for event."[20] Here there is no infinite distance between the order of nature and the order of grace, and indeed Schleiermacher's understanding contains elements in it that reflect an earlier patristic and medieval understanding. Ralph Del Colle comments on this position that it "was quite in harmony with a strong tradition that emphasized the *miracula interiora*, almost to the exclusion or insignificance of the *miracula exteriora* apart from interior faith."[21] Arguably, as we shall note in our final chapter on miracles in contemporary theology, if something like the position of David Hume reflects the regnant philosophical point of view, something like the position of Friedrich Schleiermacher remains the theological consensus. "Seeing miracles" is an act of faith, of religious interiority, and the external verification of the miraculous is secondary at best.

CHAPTER 7

MIRACLES IN CONTEMPORARY THEOLOGY

Some Snapshots

Few theological questions are treated so unsatisfactorily as the question of miracles. Discussion moves from one extreme to the other: from the extreme right, where miracles are simply accepted in a fundamentalistic sense…, to the extreme left, where miracles are rejected in principle because they are presumed to be disruptions of the inflexible laws of nature and of physics.

Richard P. McBrien[1]

The possibility of miraculous intervention, given theism, is beyond doubt.

Brian Hebblethwaite[2]

"THE ACADEMIC SNEER FACTOR"[3]

John P. Meier, the American *doyen* of scholars in pursuit of the historical Jesus, writes,

> If a full debate on the possibility and reality of miracles were to take place on American university campuses today—a highly unlikely event—such a debate would be tolerated in many quarters only with a strained smile that could hardly mask a sneer. Before any positions were articulated or discussed, the solemn creed of many university professors, especially in religion departments, would be recited *sotto voce*: "No modern educated person can accept the possibility of miracles."…In one form or another this creed has dominated American academic circles for so long that rarely does anyone bother to ask: is it *empirically* true? Please note: the question I raise is not whether modern educated persons *should* believe in miracles, but rather whether they *can* and *do* in fact believe in miracles.…Bultmann notwithstanding, the fact is that present-day educated Americans are capable of using electric lights and the "wireless" while maintaining at the same time that the Creator's powers go far beyond what human power can achieve or conceive. Whether these educated believers are consistent or reasonable in so thinking is another question. But the *fact* that they do so think is beyond dispute.[4]

There is much to ponder in Meier's words.

To help advance the discussion of the miraculous in contemporary theology it may be useful to categorize miracles in two ways: as awareness of the divine and as violation of the laws of nature. First, miracle as awareness of the divine. For the religious believer certain events and experiences can lead to a deepening awareness of the presence of God. These events and experiences are usually very ordinary, for example, a glorious sunrise or sunset, the changing seasons of the year, the sheer beauty of the natural world in all its profuse generosity. The religious believer may be led through such experiences to the conclusion that the natural world/creation, including himself or herself, is, in the words of the poet Gerard Manley Hopkins, SJ, to see the world as "charged with the grandeur of God."[5] This is what has been understood as the symbolic understanding of the miraculous referred to earlier in this book.

If as Christian believers we see the world as charged with the grandeur of God, if we see God as both the ground and the horizon of everything that exists, that is something for which to be wondrously grateful. As intelligent beings, however, we also ask questions. We are interested in exploring what it means to be a committed Christian believer in today's world. In this chapter I am going to draw together a cluster of thinkers on the miraculous with the intention of drawing out from them those insights that I believe may contribute to the building up of an intelligent Christian faith for today. As will be all too obvious to the informed reader, there are many respected and thoughtful theologians and philosophers whom I have not selected for attention. Those thinkers who follow are simply some whose work I have found particularly helpful in searching for a clearer understanding of miracle. No claim is being made to be comprehensive in treatment.

SNAPSHOT 1: RICHARD P. MCBRIEN (1936–2015)

Richard McBrien was a Catholic priest and theologian with the wonderful gift of disseminating in clear and reasonably simple terms what it means to be a Catholic Christian. In his widely used and acclaimed summary of Catholic theology, *Catholicism,* McBrien provides five theological criteria for thinking about the miracles of Jesus, criteria that would be widely shared by most centrist theologians.[6]

1. "Miracles were as important to the ministry of Jesus as his preaching." In making this statement McBrien is pointing to such passages as Luke 7:22. This is the passage in which disciples of John the Baptist are sent by him to inquire of Jesus if he is the Messiah. Luke 7:22 provides us with Jesus's response to John's disciples. "He answered them, 'Go and tell John what you have seen and heard: the blind receive their sight, the lame walk, the lepers are cleansed, the deaf hear, the dead are raised, the poor have good news brought to them." From this passage McBrien insists that miracles must be understood as related to the preaching of Jesus, and vice versa. The miracles cannot simply be dispensed with as tangential to his message.
2. "Miracles are linked with faith." McBrien emphasizes that miracles are never simply dazzling demonstrations of power on the part of Jesus but rather invitations to faith in him. Briefly but powerfully he points out that "it is possible to be present at the performance of a miracle and not see it as a miracle at all." Without a positive response

to the invitation to faith, the dynamism of the wondrous event, the miracle, seems rather empty.

3. "The miracle stories are meant to evoke faith, but not all of the stories are on the same plane." What McBrien is getting at here essentially is a fundamentalist or literalist approach. "The fundamentalist forgets that the biblical accounts are not eyewitness reports, nor scientifically tested documentation, nor historical, medical, or psychological records. They are rather unsophisticated popular narratives, entirely at the service of the proclamation of the Lordship of Jesus." In no way does he intend in these remarks to dismiss the significance of miracles. He does, however, wish to move people beyond a fundamentalist or literalist preoccupation with exact historicity toward seeing the miracles christologically.
4. "But certain events apparently did take place, and they were taken, by friend and foe alike, as marvelous in their own right." For McBrien, it is simply a fact that Jesus healed people.
5. "In the accounts of several of the miracles, too many details are given which have too little interest to have been invented and yet which are so human and true to life that this suggests the presence of an eyewitness." This is a very interesting remark. The example he posits is Mark 9:14–29, the healing of a possessed boy. McBrien's criterion might be bolstered by considering the position taken by the German Bishops' Catechism: "The healing reports frequently contain exact information about the persons involved, with names and circumstances. The throng of people, the spreading reputation of

> Jesus, the helplessness of his opponents who could not deny his deeds, the tradition of miracle accounts beginning shortly after Easter, at a time when the witnesses to the appearance of Jesus still lived—all of this cannot be understood in any other way."[7] These words are taken from a catechism commissioned by the German bishops' conference, and largely authored by theologian (later Bishop and Cardinal) Walter Kasper. They state the obvious. Yes, it is possible, argues Richard McBrien and others, to dismiss the miracles of the Gospels, but at what cost? At what cost in terms of both historical and philosophical openness? "At the very least, something significant and impressive occurred in the life and ministry of Jesus, over and above his preaching and teaching. He had an impact on people—the sick, the troubled, the bereaved—in a way that clearly set him apart from his contemporaries. Indeed, he himself pointed to his good works as moments in which the power of God operated in him and through him."[8]

McBrien's thinking does not take up all the challenges and issues regarding miracles, but regarding the New Testament and the miraculous activity attributed to Jesus he makes a very good beginning.

SNAPSHOT 2: TERENCE L. NICHOLS (1941–2014)

Terence Nichols was a professor of systematic theology at the University of St. Thomas in St. Paul, Minnesota. He had a particular interest in the relationship between science and faith and had a longstanding interest in miracles and their theology, his 1988 PhD dissertation at Marquette University having been "Miracles as Sign of the Good Creation." "Miracles are signs (not proofs) that nature exists within a higher order, an order of love and the fidelity of God. Just as divine grace heals and elevates the human intellect and will, so miracles elevate the activities of physical nature....In a miracle, nature becomes transparent to its divine ground, like a window opening onto a higher state of being. Another way of putting this is that miracles are like sacraments: they are visible events in which the divine presence shines forth."[9]

Nichols was opposed to a naïve interventionist view of God: "Nothing could be more repellent, both scientifically and theologically, than a God who capriciously intervenes to heal this person while ignoring that, or who arbitrarily interrupts natural processes to produce a 'wonder' to astonish the multitudes."[10] It is difficult right away not to find oneself being distanced from the view of God described here. It seems to pit science against faith and theology. Immediately, Nichols grasps the nettle. As Nichols develops his perspective, however, he refuses this disjunction. Instead, he argues that "the idea of miracle as a 'violation' is misleading," and he proposes the notion of miracle "as an event, caused partly by God, which is consistent with, but yet transcends, natural processes."[11] So, against naturalism he accepts that miracles do in fact occur. "They are signs that nature is not all there is, but that it exists within a more comprehensive, divine context."[12]

Nichols recognizes that skepticism about miracles came from both Deism and the Enlightenment. "[Nature] became understood as a more or less closed system, in which God could only intervene from the outside, as it were, as a mechanic would intervene to alter the workings of a clock or watch [a favorite metaphor of the Deists]."[13] Nichols believes that there is extensive evidence for miracles in the modern world and, further, that this closed view of a "naturalistic" empirical science is itself hardly scientific. It itself does not seem impartially open to evidence.

He develops his argument by way of four points:

1. The evidence for miracles is both respectable and worthy of our attention.
2. The definition of David Hume that miracles are "violations of the laws of nature" is misleading both in terms of science and in terms of theology.
3. Miracles should be understood as signs of divine action, action that does not violate nature so much as perfect it within the divine context.
4. A more adequate understanding of miracle contributes to the contemporary discussion about the nature of God's action in the world, a discussion that is to the fore in both contemporary science and theology.

The evidence for miracles is both respectable and worthy of our attention. Recognizing that miracles in the Scriptures are heavily overladen with theological symbolism, Nichols begins looking for evidence in the modern world. He fixes on the examples afforded by Lourdes. His first example is that of Dr. Alexis Carrell, a French surgeon from Lyons. In 1902 Carrell traveled to Lourdes to investigate the phenomenon of miracles, or, perhaps better, the extraordinary healings reported there. He himself did not believe in the miraculous. A young girl, Marie Bailly, who was dying of tuberculosis, was put into his care. This young girl, contrary to all expectations, was healed at Lourdes. The doctor testified to this—he had no other explanation for her recovery—and his testimony is available at the Lourdes Medical Bureau. As a result of his newfound openness to miracles, Carrell was informed that the Lyons Medical School was closed to him, and after leaving for America and joining the Rockefeller Institute, he received the Nobel prize in physiology and medicine in 1912.

Nichols provides another example from Lourdes. A twenty-nine-year-old Belgian woman, Joachime Dehant, suffering from a massive gangrenous ulcer on her right leg, found that the ulcer was cured after bathing in the waters at Lourdes. This cure was attested by physicians at Lourdes as well as by the people at home who knew her and by her own Belgian physicians. The only reasonable conclusion was that a miracle had taken place. Nichols recognizes that it is all too easy to let wish fulfillment, autosuggestion, or superstition enter the analysis. Yet it is very difficult, a priori, he maintains to dismiss such reports. He also recognizes that within the tradition of Catholicism one does not immediately jump to the explanation of the miraculous with respect to these events. "At least within Roman Catholicism," he says, "no event will be claimed to be miraculous if it can possibly be explained by natural causes."[14] How such events and reports are to be explained is another thing. At this point, Nichols is content to note that they are at least worthy of our consideration as intelligent and impartial investigators.

Miracles are violations of the laws of nature. Here, points two and three are treated together. As he moves into a consideration of David Hume's description of miracle, Nichols notes that the two Lourdes miracles that he has cited did not happen instantaneously. Each of them was, in his words, "a greatly accelerated natural process."[15] This is something that has been noted by other observers. If such accounts can be regarded as trustworthy, then miracles are less a violation of nature so much as they work around nature, working through nature to heal nature. "In this respect, [divine] action in miracles is similar to its action in what theologians call grace, which does not work against nature, but builds on nature, healing and perfecting it."[16] This point of view certainly stands as an alternative to the notion of miracle as a violation of nature. "The natural world, as described by science, is not all there is to reality. Rather, the universe exists in a wider context, which theists call a divine context. God transcends nature and holds nature in being, so that we might say (to use a spatial metaphor) that nature exists in God. Thus nature is not a system that is closed to the possibility of divine influence, but is open to it."[17] In most ordinary circumstances, then, God works through the laws of nature, but in some very rare events nature becomes "transparent to its divine ground, and behaves in extraordinary ways."[18] He considers the resurrection of Jesus such an event. "The resurrected body of Jesus (if it is/was really the same body that died, but in a transformed state, as traditional Christianity affirmed) is also within the capacities of nature, but a nature transformed by grace or divine activity."[19] Contra David Hume, miracles thus understood do not violate nature but transform it in some fashion. Miracles are not God working alone, as it were, but God working through nature or in cooperation with nature. This is quite different from the idea of God working against nature.

Even if this is accepted, it does not immediately and necessarily lead to the notion of *God* working. It would be quite possible, for example, for a scientist to claim that there simply is no known natural explanation for this event. It is also possible, he admits, that what has been regarded previously as miraculous may one day be explained when a more thorough and comprehensive understanding of nature and its workings is available.

The normal context, of course, for the occurrence of miracle is that of faith in God and prayer. From that point of view Nichols argues there are two possible ways of understanding

God's action in a miracle. The first is to claim that God responds to prayer, faith, and holiness in a person or a group by way of miraculous action. The second is to suggest that God's activity or energy "is always and everywhere available, like an extended field or supporting context."[20] This field or supporting context would be accessible to those who open themselves up to the reality of God through faith, through prayer, and through holiness of life. Nichols concludes this part of his argument in the following way:

> The models are complementary, and either without the other is incomplete. The first model explains the fact that many miracles seem to be responses to prayer. But the first model by itself is open to the objection: Why doesn't God heal everyone who prays? It may be that the reason is that to access the divine energy, it is necessary to be surrendered to God in faith and prayer, and that few people are. It is not that God plays favorites and rewards those who grovel the most. It is that those who are not deeply surrendered to God cannot access his power because they are not tuned in. For God to act in our lives, we must be receptive, and if we are not, God cannot act as fully as God might otherwise.[21]

This is a complex argument. What exactly would it mean to be deeply surrendered to God in faith and prayer? Does this account take into consideration good people who for environmental reasons (e.g., being brought up in nonreligious contexts and circumstances) would not necessarily know what it means to be deeply surrendered to God in faith and prayer? While one feels a certain sympathy with Nichols, at this point his argument is not deeply satisfying.

A more adequate understanding of miracle contributes to the contemporary discussion about the nature of God's action in the world, a discussion that is to the fore in both science and theology. It hardly needs to be pointed out that a scientist could approach miracles as illusions, or coincidences, or perhaps due to some (at this time) unknown law of nature. This position is tantamount to claiming that there is no such thing as miracles, but they are simply events that stand out from what we take to be normal. For Nichols, however, "This is a hypothesis that remains to be proven."[22] He is aware that not all theologians believe in miracles, but for those who do there is a two-step process in their discernment. First, can this supposed miracle be explained entirely and satisfactorily in terms of natural causation? Second, did this supposed miracle occur within the context of faith and prayer? If no is the answer to the first question, and yes is the answer to the second question, then the theologian may conclude that it may be a miracle. In other words, for the theologian to reach a theologically adequate conclusion, both the world of science/the quest for natural causes and the world of theology/faith come into play. It is not one at the expense of the other, but both cooperating.

Naturalism is the position that everything is explainable in terms of natural causes alone. Naturalism takes two forms—a maximal one that insists that only matter and the laws of nature actually exist, and a minimal one that insists on the existence of God above and beyond, as it were, matter and the laws of nature, but insists equally emphatically that "the chain of natural causality" is never interfered with or broken by God. Contrary to both forms of naturalism is the position of Nichols, that is, that "supernatural causality acting within the context of nature...is consistent with both forms of naturalism."[23] Nature is intrinsically open to the action of

God, though, of course, those who are locked into a naturalistic worldview will not admit this.

SNAPSHOT 3: ROWAN D. WILLIAMS (1950–)

In a small but excellent book, *Tokens of Trust: An Introduction to Christian Belief,* Anglican theologian and former archbishop of Canterbury Rowan Williams has a short but powerful treatment of miracles.[24] He opens his discussion with an experience: "Why are some prayers apparently answered and some not? I remember a vivid example from years back, when someone who had been involved in a very upbeat and confident charismatic prayer group asked why God should be thanked for finding parking spaces for members of the prayer group when he couldn't be bothered to sort out the conflict in Northern Ireland."[25] Williams remarks that it is a very good question but also that, if a genuine answer is to be found, some further thinking about God's omnipotence must be undertaken. Without going into all aspects of Williams's model of omnipotence, we may grasp the essence of it in these words: "I have been trying to suggest the picture of a God whose almighty power is more of a steady swell of loving presence, always there at work in the center of everything that is, opening the door to a future even when we can see no hope."[26] This understanding of God's omnipotence certainly seems superior to a more capricious view, or what seems a more capricious view of God's working: "A steady swell of loving presence." And, of course, a steady swell of loving presence that invites human creatures to enter that swell and to increase its intensity.

Williams goes on to summarize some thinking of St. Augustine on the question of miracles:

> Miracles were really just natural processes speeded up a bit, "fast-forwarded." This may be a bit too simple; but Augustine had got hold of something that many thinkers of the Middle Ages followed through in different ways. If God's action is always at work around us, if it's always "on hand," so to speak, we shouldn't be thinking of God's action and the processes of the world as two competing sorts of thing, jostling for space. But what if there were times when certain bits of the world's processes came together in such a way that the whole cluster of happenings became a bit more open to God's final purposes? What if the world were sometimes a bit more "transparent" to the underlying action of God?[27]

Williams's way of thinking is especially helpful. For Williams, "God has—mysteriously—made a world in which what human beings do can help or hinder what he achieves at any point in the world's history; when we give him space, through our prayerful consent to and identification with what he wants, things may happen that were otherwise unpredictable. A prejudice against any sort of miracle may be a buried uncertainty about the unfailing presence and action of the Creator, about that burning intensity of divine action that is always around us."[28] Very briefly, Williams points to the virginal conception of Jesus and to the resurrection of Jesus as illustrative of his integrated point of view. Though he does not develop this point of view at any great length, his remarks are worth noting. "Just what would the trust of Mary have had to be like for the door of life itself to open in her body? What must the faith of Jesus and his closeness to God have been that death was unable to close its doors on him and relegate him to the past?"[29] What excellent questions, stimulating us to further probing at the beginning of Jesus's life and at his end, as it were.

Thinking about miracles as natural processes in St. Augustine's and Rowan Williams's views finds some confirmation in the theology of John F. Haught (b. 1942), a former professor of theology at Georgetown University. Haught has long been interested in the interrelationship between science and theology and has published a raft of books and articles on this theme. In what some consider John Haught's summa, *The New Cosmic Story: Inside Our Awakening Universe*, we find some thinking very similar to Augustine and Williams.[30] In this fascinating and compelling story of the universe Haught takes issue with those whose horizon of intelligibility is confined to the past, to what he calls "archaeonomy." This is what he means: "Archaeonomic naturalism in principle rules out from the start the possibility that anything truly new can ever happen....Archaeonomy's signature feature is not its devotion to the analytical method of investigation but its denial that the cosmos can ever become more than what it has always been. Archaeonomic naturalists assume that in principle the universe is reducible to its primordial subatomic past."[31] Within this perspective nothing new can take place. Rather, everything is reducible to the dictatorial findings of the investigation of the past on the part of science. Haught asks the question, however, "What if the universe is still in the process of becoming?" He continues, "Only recently has science demonstrated beyond reasonable doubt that the universe is still coming into being, that nature is narrative to the core, and that the cosmic story is far from finished. Thanks to developments especially in geology, biology, and cosmology we now know that we live in a universe that is still on a long journey."[32] From an anticipatory hermeneutic, the still-expanding cosmos is moving toward a richer and more beautiful and infinitely more satisfying plenitude of being that takes the past with it. Although Haught has nothing to say about the miraculous as such, this anticipatory perspective that he advocates, an advocacy based on the twin pillars of science and religion, may itself on occasion find signals in the present. These signals would be "miracles." In other words, what is experienced here and now as the miraculous, from this anticipatory worldview, is the future fast-forwarded in the present. In an archaeonomic hermeneutic of the cosmos, with David Hume perhaps as its star performer, this is impossible in principle. In his archaeonomic principle, what has already happened in a finished universe, so to speak, determines what may or may not happen.

SNAPSHOT 4: BRIAN HEBBLETHWAITE (1939–)

Brian Hebblethwaite is an Anglican priest and theologian who spent most of his professional career teaching at the University of Cambridge. He has always had an interest in philosophy, especially philosophy in the Anglo-analytic tradition, and it is out of this tradition that he considers miracles.

"While it is hard to assess the miraculous element [in the gospel records], it is hard to deny that in Jesus of Nazareth we have to do with a charismatic healer. Even the agnostic historian E. P. Sanders, in *The Historical Figure of Jesus*, presents us with a figure, while every inch a Jew, nevertheless stands out remarkably from his Jewish background."[33] The historian, precisely as a historian, maintains Hebblethwaite, can only point to the claimed appearances of the risen Christ and also to the empty tomb tradition. He cites the historian of Jesus E. P. Sanders, who writes, "That Jesus' followers (and later Paul) had resurrection experiences is, in my judgment, a fact. What the reality was that gave rise to the experiences

I do not know."[34] Hebblethwaite continues: "The transformation of the disciples from demoralized fugitives to preachers of a new age and the emergence and spread of the Christian movement are all historical facts to which appeal is made in Christian apologetic. In our connection with the other elements in the cumulative case to which I have alluded, developed Christian doctrine attempts, among all things, to offer the best explanation of these puzzling historical facts."[35] In other words, affirming the objectivity of the resurrection events—in whatever way one wishes to define objectivity—makes better sense of the actual evidence than any alternative and reductionist naturalistic explanation.

For Brian Hebblethwaite, theologically sensitive objection to miracles includes three strands:

> In the first place, a mature theology has to take account of scientific knowledge and relate its understanding of God's way with the world to modern knowledge about the manner in which the created world operates. In the second place, the problem of evil requires recognition of the reasons why God has to respect the structures of his creation.... If direct intervention, with laser beam precision, were a real possibility, its absence in innumerable cases of horrendous evil is morally inexplicable. And thirdly, a theologically sensitive understanding of divine providence operating in and through the law-governed, yet open and flexible, structures of the world makes more sense of the history of religions, and indeed of incarnation, than the postulation of direct, unmediated intervention.[36]

Hebblethwaite considers the resurrection, along with his mentor Austin Farrer, as "not a miracle like any other. It is a unique manifestation within this world of the transition God makes for us out of this way of being into another."[37] In Hebblethwaite's own words: "The way in which God grants an anticipatory manifestation of the transformation of the old creation into the new is not a paradigm for the understanding of God's action in history. It has effects in history (the appearances and the empty tomb); but, as already argued, the event itself is, in the nature of the case, metahistorical."[38]

Hebblethwaite's reasoned conclusion is as follows:

> Appeals to history, then, do constitute an integral part of Christian apologetic, and indeed of critical reflection in support of the Christian faith. But, I repeat, these tentative, exploratory, probabilistic, even hypothetical, reasonings do not belong to the foundations of Christianity. Committed participation in the convictional community of the Christian church has its own internal warrant.... Christian belief is undoubtedly founded, if true, on God's action in history, most particularly in the Incarnation and the Resurrection. This conviction belongs to the basic belief structure of Christianity as a lived religion. But probabilistic, evidentialist, cumulative reason of the sort examined in this book may also be helpful for answering doubts and commending the faith to others. Without any such support, individual Christians might well be vulnerable to loss of faith, and the church's apologetic would have to be replaced simply by proclamation. Not that there is anything wrong with proclamation. All I am claiming is that there is a place for reasoning, irrespective of commitment, too.[39]

The value of Hebblethwaite's approach, as briefly summarized here, is the support it offers to the faith of individual Christians. He is an apologist for Christian faith. In his apologetics, as in any form of Christian apologetics, there is a certain tension straddling reason and faith. There is no way finally to resolve this tension, but reflecting deeply within the tension between reason and faith can help to sustain and build up Christian faith.

SNAPSHOT 5: HANS KÜNG (1928–)

In spite of his difficulties with the hierarchical church and the church authorities, Hans Küng has been a premier and eminently successful apologist for Christianity. In his 2007 book, *The Beginning of All Things: Science and Religion*, Küng gives a brief but clear account of miracle as he understands it.

He comes at an understanding of the biblical miracles with all the apparatus of contemporary hermeneutical theory, but he is emphatic that he does not want to destroy anyone's faith. "I do not want to violate the religious feelings of anyone for whose belief in God the miracles understood literally are important. I want to give a helpful answer to those modern men and women for whom the miracles are an obstacle to their faith."[40] His project, therefore, has to do with presenting an approach to the miraculous for modern people who find the notion of the miraculous problematic for their Christian faith. That is very clear.

Right away, Küng describes the difference between a biblical approach to reality during the times when the Holy Scriptures were written and a contemporary approach.

> People did not think scientifically, and so they did not understand the miracles as breaking the laws

> of nature; they did not understand them as a violation of seamless causal connections. So nowhere in the Hebrew Bible and the New Testament is a distinction made between miracles that correspond to the laws of nature and others that break them. For every event through which God revealed his power was regarded at that time as a miracle, as a "sign," as a mighty act of God. God was at work everywhere, the creator and primal ground.[41]

From this broad perspective and in the light of historical and literary critical approaches to the Bible, miracles understood as breaking the laws of nature cannot be demonstrated, "and those who think they can be demonstrated bear the burden of proof."[42]

His conclusion, therefore, is this: "The miracles stand in the Bible as metaphors, just as in poetry metaphors too do not set out to overturn the laws of nature."[43] This perspective generates an understanding of miracle as not in competition with the scientific and technological understanding of reality. Narratives about miracles are meant to be pointers to God's action in the world and, moreover, pointers that require faith in God as their ground. "[The miracles] proclaim not an unchanging unworldly and unhistorical God who unfeelingly leaves the world and human beings to their fate, but a God who gets involved with the destinies of the world, and commits himself for the people and for individuals....a God who does not leave the world and human beings alone, who does not make history a dark, ominous fate for people by the connection of events but can be recognized in faith."[44]

Needless to say, this raises the question of how God acts in the world. "It would be an all-too-external anthropomorphic notion to think that God as Lord and King 'controlled' or 'guided' events, even those that are apparently chance, even the indeterminate subatomic processes."[45] He advocates an understanding of God in these terms: "an understanding of reality in which God as Spirit is in the world and the world is in God, transcendence in immanence."[46] His language here is very close to the language of process theology, or what has been termed "panentheism." "God's spirit works in the regular structures of the world but is not identical with them."[47] In these words Küng is able to affirm God's utter and transcendent priority while simultaneously affirming his immanence. God's Spirit is not at work in gaps in the world process. God and the world are not to be understood as competing finite causalities; "they are in each other. If God really is the all-embracing infinite spiritual primal ground, primal support, and primal meaning of the world and human beings, it becomes clear that God does not lose anything if human beings in their finitude win, but that God wins when human beings win."[48] Endorsing the work of scientist-priest-theologian John Polkinghorne, Küng says,

> The actual equilibrium between chance and necessity, contingency and possibility that we perceive seems to correspond to the will of a patient and subtle creator who is content to pursue his aims by initiating the process and by accepting that degree of vulnerability and uncertainty that always characterizes the gift of freedom through love.[49]

This leads Küng to the conclusion that "most miracles take place for believers not in the cosmos but in the human heart, where God's spirit is at work."[50]

SNAPSHOT 6: THOMAS JAY OORD (1965–)

Thomas Jay Oord is a process theologian. His ultimate terms of reference, therefore, are to be found within the metaphysical categories of process theism. "We must resist the temptation," he believes, "to envision God as capable of coercion. Theologies that present God as capable of coercion at the eschaton do not function adequately as theologies of love."[51] Admittedly, he is talking about the eschaton, the end of all things. He posits a cogent point about the noncoercive activity of God at the eschaton:

> A "kick-butt" God gives up on kenotic love and resorts to coercion at the end. There is no reason to trust that the God who has coercive capacities but fails to use them consistently throughout history is a God whom we should trust to express love at the end. Such a God is not trustworthy. If God has coercive powers, why wait to use them? The God capable of coercion at the end of all things is culpable for failing to prevent evil throughout history. The end—guaranteed victory—does not justify the means—divine coercion.[52]

If divine coercion is not in place, eschatology is shot through with hope. "Essential kenosis theology affirms Christian hope rests ultimately in the steadfast, kenotic, and non-coercive love of God. This hope has at least three dimensions. Our hope is God's loving reign in this life, in the afterlife, and in the fulfillment of all things. Hope, in all of these dimensions, plays a crucial role in the Christian witness and well placed confidence to live lives of love."[53] This is the bottom line for Oord.

If the word *intervention* means that God enters history or creation from outside, for Oord this is impossible. "An omnipresent God never needs to intervene, because God is always already present in every situation. God is never 'outside,' in the sense that creation functions independently of God's continual creating and sustaining. The God already present to all things at all times does not need to interrupt creation to act miraculously."[54] If this impasse is to be avoided, it is necessary to find a more adequate way of thinking about God's love and power than that which is or traditionally has been widespread.

This leads Oord to think of miracles as "moments or events in which the loving activity of an almighty God dramatically affects a creature or situation. We should deem these dramatic moments 'miracles,' because they promote overall well-being and remind us that God sometimes works in spectacular, but non-coercing, ways."[55] We need the ongoing witness of God's miraculous love constantly to remind us of God's being at work in creation and thus to engender human hope. God's love varies both in intensity and in form and should not be understood as "a steady-state, impersonal, or homogeneous force."[56] Alternatively, "God lovingly interacts with creatures, gives and receives, and influences and is influenced by others."[57] Thus, Oord argues that God's loving activity "oscillates," that is to say that "God's will is more or less expressed as creatures respond well or poorly to God's freedom-providing love."[58] This takes him to his understanding of miracle: "When creatures promote overall well-being in an extraordinary way, God's love, which inspired and empowered this extraordinary behavior, is most evident. We witness a miracle....While God always loves, some events display that love spectacularly and others do not."[59]

Of course, this seems to lead us to a dilemma. Does God choose to love some persons and situations more than others so that miracles occur? Oord eschews this point of view. God's nature as love is simply never absent. But God's loving causal effectiveness "oscillates as creatures cooperate to greater or lesser degree."[60] "God's oscillating and diverse love depends in part upon God's own essence as love, in part upon the particular forms and expressions God chooses when loving to the utmost, and in part upon creaturely responses."[61] "Miracles reveal the profound love of God and profound creaturely cooperation."[62] As examples he points to the miracles in Mark 5:34; Matthew 9:29; and Mark 8:22–25. In each instance there is an element of creaturely cooperation in the narrative. So, Oord concludes that "lack of creaturely cooperation keeps miracles from occurring."[63] The supreme gospel instance that demonstrates his conclusion is afforded by Matthew 13:58, in which Jesus cannot do many miracles in his hometown because of the lack of cooperation, that is to say, "because of their unbelief." "A loving God invites creatures to cooperate in the miracles God intends for them and for others."[64]

Thinking and reflecting within the ambience of process theology, Oord maintains that, however difficult it may be to observe empirically, all creation has a measure of freedom. This is how he puts it:

> Being lovingly present to all things means that God is also present to bodily organs, cells, nonhumans, and less complex creatures. Just as God lovingly provides freedom/agency to humans, God also provides freedom and agency to other complex and simple creatures and organisms. Of course, the agency and perhaps freedom of simple organisms and cells is vastly less than what humans are given. But even at the micro level, God does not coerce. When simpler organisms, cells, and other creatures

respond well to God's loving activities, miracles can occur.[65]

SNAPSHOT 7: THOMAS E. HOSINSKI, CSC (1946–)

Thomas Hosinski taught theology at the University of Portland in Oregon for many years and has, since the time of his doctoral dissertation at the University of Chicago, had a keen interest in reconciling the categories of process philosophy with Catholic theology. In his book *The Image of the Unseen God,* he offers a very brief consideration of miracles against the backdrop of the qualified process philosophy/theology that he espouses. Hosinski writes,

> The testimony of Christian religious experience, and that of other religious traditions as well, holds that miraculous events do occur. The Gospels present Jesus as one who worked miracles. Even more important, the heart of the Christian gospel proclamation includes the miracle of the resurrection of Jesus from the dead. It does not seem that the Christian tradition can easily give up the claim that miraculous events occur, despite the fact that the intellectual history of the last three centuries in the West has led to even many Christian theologians to "demythologize" or spiritualize such claims, including the claim for the resurrection of Jesus.[66]

At least in principle, Hosinski displays a certain openness to the miraculous. He notes that "in this matter everything depends on how one defines what a miracle is."[67] His interdisciplinary interest in science and theology leads him to recognize how so much depends on the actual definition of a miracle. "One of the keys to understanding miracles in a new way resides in the revised understanding of the laws of nature made possible by contemporary science....These laws predict not what must occur, but rather the likelihood or probability of events....With regard to such statistical laws, a miracle may be defined not as a violation of the laws of nature but as an extremely unlikely or improbable event."[68] There is one important metaphysical consequence of this change of definition: "One can never rule out the possibility of an unlikely or improbable event. So long as that event is not impossible, but is merely highly unlikely, our metaphysics would have to allow for the possibility of its occurrence."[69] Based on the metaphysics of Alfred North Whitehead, Hosinski affirms "the possibility of miracles understood as extremely improbable events." He continues, "If God acts through the presentation of possibilities and lures actual agents toward actualizing the possibility God values most highly, there is no theoretical obstacle to affirming that on occasion God can lure actual agents into actualizing an extremely improbable possibility."[70] He then offers his understanding of the resurrection of Jesus on the basis of this understanding of miracle:

> The resurrection of Jesus from the dead could be understood as an extremely improbable but nevertheless possible objective historical event, not just a subjective event occurring in the hearts and minds of his disciples, as so many theologians have proposed. How exactly the resurrection occurred I cannot suggest, but I would offer the judgment that God elicited life out of an inanimate world once before and I think it not impossible for God to have elicited life out of death in this instance,

> raising Jesus to new and transformed life as a promise and revelation of what awaits us all.[71]

Hosinski's position is interesting here. On the one hand, he readily acknowledges the metaphysical improbability of the resurrection of Jesus, and, on the other hand, he notes that epistemologically it cannot be ruled a priori as impossible. Constructively, he concludes that the account of the resurrection of Jesus to new life in God is to be trusted as revealing the Christian hope for the future of everyone.

SNAPSHOT 8: GABRIEL DALY, OSA (1928–)

In a brief but profound chapter of his book *Asking the Father*, Irish systematic theologian Gabriel Daly tackles the issue of miracles. The chapter is entitled "The World in Which We Do Our Praying."[72] Primitive human beings did not distinguish between the seen and the unseen worlds, both of which "belonged to the one mysterious theater into which he was born, lived his precarious life, and died."[73] This way of looking at things began to change between 800 BC and 200 BC, the period of the higher religions, when human beings began to ask fundamental questions about the meaning of life and reality. This Daly refers to as the first great revolution in human understanding. The second revolution occurred between the beginning of the sixteenth century and the end of the seventeenth century, introducing a new cosmology with the discoveries of Copernicus and Galileo. These discoveries challenged the worldview that was informed by Aristotelianism, on the one hand, and the Bible, on the other. A rift developed between the prevailing Christian worldview and the emerging scientific worldview. Daly points out that scientists who were also Christian believers of a sort, like Isaac Newton, tried to effect a reconciliation. Daly summarizes the weaknesses of this attempted reconciliation as follows: "With the best will in the world, Newton had created what is today often described as 'the God of the gaps,' i.e., a God who is invoked to fill the provisional and temporary gaps in scientific knowledge. As science filled more and more of these gaps, Newton's God was progressively banished from the universe and was replaced by nature."[74] Thus, phenomena that had traditionally been attributed to God's special intervention in the world could not be explained along scientific lines without recourse to God, and obviously, the reality of the miraculous was questioned. What had appeared as miraculous before was now explicable in terms of science.

Much depends, of course, on how one understands miracle. "The neo-scholastic definition, which prevailed in the Catholic Church before Vatican II, was unequivocal: a miracle is an event which takes place outside, and normally in contradiction of, the course of nature. This definition postulates an intervention of God not merely within the universe he had created but in contravention of the laws he has given it."[75] Seeing God's presence and action in this way, suspending or bypassing the laws of nature, is very problematic. In Daly's terms, "It leaves too many problems unsolved while creating new and gratuitous ones. The sheer inequity and the seemingly capricious character of sporadic divine interventions sets up serious questions about the care of God for all his creation. Why are some favored and others not?"[76] Daly points out that the conventionally pious answer to this question is that God knows what is best for each person and, therefore, when to intervene and when not. The image of God that lies behind this conventionally pious response is not very convincing. It smacks of a patronizing and condescending "father knows best" approach to this enormously complex issue.

Daly points out, however, that there is an alternative way to approach the issue, and that is to see God's action as "no less present in the processes we understand scientifically than in those we do not understand. A beautiful sunrise, the smile of a baby, or a Mozart symphony can be miraculous for someone who experiences them in a faith-inspired way. The concept of miracle is a religious not a scientific one."[77] This notion that the concept of miracle is a religious not a scientific concept seems to suggest that miracles are not open to scientific observation and investigation. They are of a different order of truth. "To the truly believing man or woman any event or phenomenon can be miraculous in that it leads to wonder at the glory and beauty of it all. A miracle thus understood is God's grace lighting up ordinary events in such a way as to provoke wonder or a sense of awe. Whether or not the event or phenomenon can be, either then or later, explained by scientific means is unimportant."[78] And so, Daly insists, "Paradoxically, it is concern with miracle which may most serve to blind us to God's constant and never failing presence and action in the world."[79]

SNAPSHOT 9: LUKE TIMOTHY JOHNSON (1943–)

The very final paragraph of Luke Timothy Johnson's book *Miracles* reads as follows:

> For believers, the truth is that the living God will continue to manifest his presence and power within creation. The issue is not that truth. The issue is whether humans will have ears to hear the word that God seeks to express, or eyes to perceive the signs and wonders that God uses to draw attention

> to the truth about humans and their world. The church ought to be the place in the world where God's continuing self-revelation is discerned, accelerated, and embodied. But if the church's members, and above all its ministers, share the secular world view that excludes God from consideration, or at best are double-minded, trying to fit Christianity into a frame that the gospel itself refutes, then the church will be less able to be church. The church's greatest gift and its mightiest challenge is to declare God's self-revelation within the world that God brings into being, the One from whom creation derives, and the One to whom creation is ordered. Failure at this is utter failure.[80]

The paragraph summarizes with great clarity the core message of Johnson's excellent and indeed inspirational book. The book begins with his conviction that Christians have permitted Enlightenment epistemology, "demonstrating the possibility, probability, or reality of miracles by using historical methods," to dominate their approach to the miraculous.[81] He weighs in against what he takes to be the skepticism of the Enlightenment over the fundamental conviction of God's presence and power in creation. The former has been allowed not only to overshadow the latter but virtually to eliminate it. "Even within a Roman Catholicism that requires the proof of miracles by those who would be designated as saints, the hierarchy exercises an almost obsessive caution with respect to the demonstration of such wonders as 'supernatural'; it tends to approach any freelance claim to the miraculous—be it Marian appearances at places like Lourdes and Fatima, or the claims to stigmata for such as Padre Pio or Therese Neumann—with the presumption of fraud or psychopathology."[82]

Throughout the book Johnson takes issue with reductionist, "secularist" approaches to Scripture and to the miraculous. He understands very well that contemporary-thinking Christians find themselves in a difficult position: "From one side they are pressed by the claims of Scripture and tradition concerning the work of the living God in the world; from every other side, they are pressed even more powerfully by the cultural assumptions of the world in which they live, assumptions that make the miraculous a problematic category."[83] His book stands as a corrective against such cultural assumptions. If God is not only the foundation but the sustaining force behind all reality, then the presence and power of God necessarily for a believer will have an epistemological priority.

In this respect, I want to align myself with this approach of Luke Timothy Johnson. If, in his words, a miracle is "a disclosure of God's presence and power in a manner and degree irreducible to the ordinary expectations for human activity," then, quite simply, allowance must be made for such disclosures.[84] A hermeneutic of generosity must win out over a hermeneutic of suspicion, and thus Scripture will be seen to reveal "this world as permeable to and penetrated by [the] divine power,"[85] and the miraculous will be seen not as "an exception to the well-established laws of nature" but rather as "the magic of God's power and presence, whose laws or logic humans must struggle to decipher."[86]

"Struggling to decipher"—that is ultimately what's at stake, and this is surely where human reason comes into play as it struggles to decipher God at work in events. If critical reason is pushed off to the sidelines, then fideism ensues. If faithful trust in God's presence and power is marginalized or eliminated, then the consequence is rationalism. A certain tension, then, must exist between faith and reason, and only the mutually critical correlation of both will yield a sane balance in the life of the individual or the community.

SNAPSHOT 10: JOHN MACQUARRIE (1919–2007)

The Scottish Anglican theologian John Macquarrie was one of the most respected and influential English-language theologians of the twentieth century, and not only in his own Anglican Communion. He had a profound influence on generations of Catholic theologians and seminarians.[87] His approach to theology is both accessible and readily intelligible, not least when it comes to miracles.[88]

"In a minimal sense, a miracle is an event that excites wonder." With this opening remark Macquarrie is referring to the linguistic origins of the English word *miracle,* that is, to the Latin verb *mirari,* meaning "to wonder, to wonder at." In a religious context, however, there is more to it than simply the excitement of wonder. "It is believed that God is in the event in some special way, that he is the author of it, and intends to achieve some special end by it." In other words, a miracle is understood in Christian terms as "an act of God."[89]

In earlier sections of his *Principles of Christian Theology,* Macquarrie recognizes that "God is present and active in the whole world-process," and, therefore, "it is clear that some happenings count for more than others, or are more important or significant than others." He does not wish to affirm that somehow everything is miracle in line with some idealist philosophers and theologians of the nineteenth century, thinkers who were desirous to avoid any notion of sporadic intervention by a God who was outside of the world. He puts it quite succinctly: "Even if all events belong within a continuous series, some stand out within the series as critical moments in its unfolding."[90] To describe every event as somehow miraculous is to evacuate the concept of any genuine meaning.

Equally, Macquarrie does not want to endorse a view of the miraculous as a break in the natural order, a break due to supernatural intervention. He regards such a view as mythological. A modern understanding of science and history makes such an interventionist view of the miraculous incredible. Inevitably, the Christian theologian comes up against "problematic events" that, though well attested, cannot be accounted for in terms of "immanent causal factors."[91] Reports of healings, for example, in the New Testament, are a good illustration of such problematic events. Macquarrie regards the healing miracles of the New Testament as more likely and credible than the so-called nature miracles. "The reason for our assigning the healing miracles this higher degree of probability is that the same kind of events are reported today from Lourdes and elsewhere."[92] Macquarrie offers some elucidation: "We simply do not understand how such events happen or what are the intricate linkages." He goes on to comment, "We cannot, in our present state of knowledge concerning nature and man, explain how these events come about." He refuses to see them as "the irruption of a supernatural agency."[93]

He comes at his understanding of miracle, then, not "in some extraordinary publicly observable event, but in God's presence and self-manifestation in the event. This is not something publicly observable, nor is it something that requires some prodigy, or breach of nature, for its occurrence."[94] The essence of the phenomenon is this presence and self-manifestation of God. Since God's acting or presence cannot be proved by publicly observable events, miracle has a certain ambiguous character. "From one point of view, the event is seen as a perfectly ordinary event; from another point of view, it is an event that opens up Being and becomes a vehicle for Being's revelation or grace or judgment or address." Immediately, of course, this raises the question whether a miracle really is being reduced to someone's "subjective apprehension" of it.[95]

As Macquarrie goes further into the matter, he introduces the notion of "focusing." This is what he means by focusing: "God's presence and activity are everywhere and always; yet we experience these intensely in particular concrete happenings, in which, as it were, they have been focused."[96] Again, this raises the question of whether the "subjective apprehension" of miracle is the all-determining factor. Macquarrie recognizes both the objective and the subjective factors. "As revelation is a movement of Being in us, and as symbols are genuinely kin to what they illuminate, so miracle is the approach and self-disclosure of Being to us in and with and through the focusing event, bringing grace or revelation or judgment as the case may be."[97]

The supreme miracle in Christian faith for Macquarrie is the incarnation of our Lord Jesus Christ. This helps provide a better understanding of this concept of miracle. From one point of view, Jesus was simply another human being. But he was so much more for the disciples and for those who followed him. "But to the disciples, this life was the focusing of the presence and action of God. Faith perceived the dimension which is not publicly observable, and could not be."[98] While faith cannot be proved or disproved simply by observation or argument, in this instance of the incarnation "it is confirmed in the community's subsequent life of faith, where the miracle of incarnation interprets the community's existence, lends meaning to it, strengthens its being."[99] In other words, he suggests that the ongoing, deeper, continually enriched life of the community "confirms" the reality of the miracle of the incarnation. "The sacraments, for instance, are such foci." Through the example of the Eucharist, which he goes on to explain, the community finds its life ongoing, deeper, and continually enriched. This is why "talk of the 'miracle of the mass' is not just superstitious talk but points to the focusing of the divine presence of the Eucharist.... Miracle is not magic, but the focusing of holy Being's presence and action amid the events, things, and persons of the world, and this has the highest reality."[100]

CONCLUSION

This chapter has outlined the points of view of ten respected Christian systematic theologians from different ecclesial traditions. Two things seem to emerge from their different points of view. First, uniformly all of them reject what might be called an interventionist point of view on God's part regarding miracles. An interventionist point of view seems to suggest that God is normally absent from his creation. All the above theologians insist on God's presence in and to his creation, his immanence in creation. Second, while there are family resemblances between some of these theologians, they share no universally accepted metaphysics. There is, of course, no revealed metaphysics. In that sense, the theologian must think things through as best he or she can, using the best philosophical wisdom available. Inevitably, that means, as can be seen in the above selection, that there will be a plurality of views, and, it must be noted, a plurality of views held by committed Christian theologians.

CHAPTER 8

CONCLUSION

> You know, children, miracles are not so much about changes that happen out there in the world, but about changes that happen in the way we see the world. They're about changes in our own hearts, which help us to see that everything is a miracle....Miracles happen all the time, to people who know how to look at the world.
>
> Fr. John[1]

The words that open this conclusion are taken from a homily by Fr. John in a liturgy for schoolchildren during Lent. The priest is the central character in an outstanding novel by theologian Tina Beattie entitled *The Good Priest*. Fr. John is preparing the children as best he can for the great celebration of the resurrection of Christ at Easter, and he wants to anchor the miracle of the resurrection in the experience of the children. This is the context for his homily in the novel. I am deliberately using the fictitious Fr. John's point of view because he is saying something enormously important. In chapter 5 of this book there was a recognition of the importance of "interior miracles," that is, the daily and moral-spiritual miracles that take place in the human heart within the process of ongoing conversion. That is what Fr. John is witnessing to in his homily. If the point of life is about communion with God here and now—"in God we live, and move, and have our being"—being drawn to completion gracefully by God after death, then seeing the miraculous is primarily and foundationally about seeing God drawing us to himself every day, invisibly but powerfully, unobtrusively but really. Miracles are about learning how to see the world-with-God and about letting our hearts be changed. That seems to me the absolute bottom line.

Nevertheless, a little more needs to be said. There are lots of books on miracles offering a range of viewpoints and interpretations, all of which find their roots in a variety of philosophical and theological presuppositions. This little book on miracles obviously reflects the bias of the author, that is, his philosophical and theological presuppositions. Needless to say, not everyone will share either these presuppositions or this bias, something mentioned in the preface. However, one reaches the point in theological thinking where one has to say, "This is where I stand. Having thought through the issues as best I can, this is my understanding."

That understanding may be summarized in the following statements:

1. Christian faith demands the fundamental acknowledgment that God is always present and active throughout creation. God is never absent. In that sense there can be no divine "interventions" or "interruptions," as though God were not already present.
2. Accounts of "miracles"—recognizing, of course, various definitions of the term—abound throughout the Bible and the Christian tradition. Attention must be paid intelligently to such matters as

literary genre, the probable situations in which miraculous narratives arose, and the intention of the authors. Theological motives are always more foundational than historiography, although that does not mean that miraculous narratives do not contain accurate historical recollection.

3. Living in a world in which the Enlightenment has happened means that a Christian must use critical understanding of all the doctrines, events, and phenomena of the Christian religion. We may be critical of the critiques of the Enlightenment, but we cannot think as if it has not happened.
4. Living out of a committed Christian faith and at the same time reflecting critically on what that faith means, the miracles of the Old Testament are best understood as cult-legends that enable people to perceive the ever-present and ever-active God or folktales that help to confirm religious identity and conviction.
5. Living out of a committed Christian faith and at the same time reflecting critically on what that faith means, the healing miracles of Jesus appear to be well-founded historically—however they are to be understood—but the nature miracles are better understood as theological/christological interpretations, designed to confirm religious identity and conviction.
6. With respect to modern accounts of miracles, with John Macquarrie, "We cannot, in our present state of knowledge concerning nature and man, explain how these events come about," but they should be seen not as "the irruption of a

supernatural agency" but as manifestations, in and through faith, of the God who is Love.

7. Finally, espousing the perspective of Rowan Williams and John Haught, the miraculous may be seen as the anticipation in our present world and experience of an indescribable future cosmic fullness, a fullness that Christians might describe as the Parousia.

Undoubtedly these summary statements will leave some Christian believers unconvinced and desirous of offering alternative explanatory accounts, and this takes us back to reflections and sentiments expressed in the preface to this book. Something of a pastorally persuasive position may be found in some comments of the late New Testament scholar Reginald H. Fuller about New Testament miracles, but we could also say about miracles more generally, "Could we come to a gentleman's agreement about this question, which so divides Christians today? Could we agree to live and let live, and say to the fundamentalist, 'All right, you continue taking for granted the historicity of the miraculous draft of fishes. Intellectual integrity compels me to doubt it. But for both of us that is neither here nor there.' Whether we take its historicity for granted or not, the real point lies, *as it did for the evangelist*, elsewhere."[2] By "elsewhere" Fuller means the deeper, theological, christological, and ecclesial insights enshrined in the narratives. That surely is the nub of the issue. As Gabriel Daly, mentioned in chapter 7, put it so succinctly, "The true Christian challenge is not necessarily to share theological convictions, but to get along together in spite of their differences."[3]

NOTES

CHAPTER 1

1. Ninian Smart, *Philosophers and Religious Truth*, 2nd ed. (London: SCM Press, 1969), 25.

2. Kenneth Woodward, *Making Saints* (New York: Simon and Schuster, 1990), 200.

3. For a good introduction to the miraculous and other religious traditions, one might consult the essays in part 3 of Graham H. Twelftree, ed., *The Cambridge Companion to Miracles* (Cambridge: Cambridge University Press, 2011), and especially the essays by Fiona Bowie, Gavin Flood, David Thomas, Rupert Gethin, and Kenneth Seeskin.

4. Smart, *Philosophers and Religious Truth*, 26.

5. G. F. Woods, "The Evidential Value of the Biblical Miracles," in *Miracles: Cambridge Studies in Their Philosophy and History*, ed. C. F. D. Moule (New York: Morehouse-Barlow, 1965), 21.

6. Joseph T. Lienhard, *The Bible, the Church, and Authority* (Collegeville, MN: Liturgical Press, 1995), 6–7.

7. Joseph Houston, *Reported Miracles* (Cambridge: Cambridge University Press, 1994), 3.

8. John P. Meier, *A Marginal Jew*, vol. 2, *Mentor, Message, and Miracles* (New York and London: Doubleday, 1994), 511–1038. The definition is from page 512.

9. Louis Monden, *Signs and Wonders: A Study of the Miraculous Element in Religion* (New York: Desclée, 1966), 7. The "high quarters" to which he refers here is a warning given by Cardinal

Alfredo Ottaviani of the Holy Office (now the Congregation for the Doctrine of the Faith), reported in the *Tablet*, February 24, 1951, 144–45.

10. Meier, *A Marginal Jew*, 514.

11. John Cottingham, *Why Believe?* (New York and London: Continuum, 2009), 79.

CHAPTER 2

1. John L. McKenzie, *Dictionary of the Bible* (Milwaukee: Bruce, 1965), 578.

2. Walter L. Moberly, "Miracles in the Hebrew Bible," in *The Cambridge Companion to Miracles*, ed. Graham H. Twelftree (Cambridge: Cambridge University Press, 2011), 57.

3. Moberly, "Miracles in Hebrew Bible," 58.

4. See John P. Ross, "Some Notes on Miracle in the Old Testament," in *Miracles: Cambridge Studies in Their Philosophy and History*, ed. C. F. D. Moule (New York: Morehouse Barlow, 1965), 52. Ross continues on 59: "The most humdrum tactical stroke, the most brilliant strategy, the most astonishing coincidence (and in course of time what appears to the modern mind the most incredible exaggeration), were all acts of God, differing, perhaps, in magnificence, but not in credibility."

5. Luke Timothy Johnson, *Miracles: God's Presence and Power in Creation* (Louisville, KY: Westminster John Knox Press, 2018), 79, my emphasis.

6. Johnson, *Miracles*, 92.

7. Johnson, *Miracles*, 93.

8. Gerald O'Collins, *Inspiration* (New York: Oxford University Press, 2018), 28.

9. Michael D. Coogan, "Joshua," in *The New Jerome Biblical Commentary*, 2nd ed., ed. R. E. Brown, J. A. Fitzmyer, and R. E. Murphy (Englewood Cliffs, NJ: Prentice-Hall, 1990), 111.

10. John J. Collins, *Introduction to the Hebrew Bible*, 2nd ed. (Minneapolis: Fortress Press, 2014), 110.

11. Collins, *Introduction to Hebrew Bible*, 112.

12. Colin Humphreys, *The Miracles of Exodus: A Scientist's Discovery of the Extraordinary Natural Causes of the Biblical Stories* (New York: Continuum, 2003), 5, as cited by John J. Collins.

13. John Coventry, *Christian Truth* (New York: Paulist Press, 1975), 22.

14. Barnabas Lindars, "Elijah, Elisha and the Gospel Miracles," in *Miracles: Cambridge Studies in Their Philosophy and History*, ed. C. F. D. Moule (London: A. R. Mowbray, 1965), 64–65. Lindars also contributed the article "Miracle" in *A New Dictionary of Christian Theology*, ed. Alan Richardson and John Bowden (London: SCM Press, 1983), 370–72.

15. Lindars, "Elijah, Elisha and the Gospel Miracles," 66.

16. McKenzie, *Dictionary of the Bible*, 579.

17. Paul Ternant, "Miracle," in *Dictionary of Biblical Theology*, ed. Xavier Léon-Dufour, SJ (New York: Desclée, 1967), 318.

18. Johnson, *Miracles*, 114.

19. Lindars, "Elijah, Elisha and Gospel Miracles," 75.

20. Lindars, "Elijah, Elisha and Gospel Miracles," 67.

21. Lindars, "Elijah, Elisha and Gospel Miracles," 69–70, notes that the feeding of a hero by animals is a well-known motif in folklore, e.g., the legend of Romulus and Remus. He also notes that the word *ravens* in Hebrew may be pointed differently and read as "Arabs." In Lindars's judgment, while this reading is not impossible, it reflects the modern tendency to provide a naturalistic explanation of the event.

22. Lindars, "Elijah, Elisha and Gospel Miracles," 70.

23. Lindars, "Elijah, Elisha and Gospel Miracles," 70.

24. Jerome T. Walsh and Christopher T. Begg, "1–2 Kings," in Brown, Fitzmyer, and Murphy, *The New Jerome Biblical Commentary*, 171.

25. Lindars, "Elijah, Elisha and Gospel Miracles," 71.

26. Lindars, "Elijah, Elisha and Gospel Miracles," 72.

27. Lindars, "Elijah, Elisha and Gospel Miracles," 72–73.

28. Lindars, "Elijah, Elisha and Gospel Miracles," 73.

29. Lindars, "Elijah, Elisha and Gospel Miracles," 73.

30. Joseph Blenkinsopp, "Miracles: Elisha and Hanina ben Dosa," in *Miracles in Jewish and Christian Antiquity*, ed. John C. Cavadini (Notre Dame, IN: University of Notre Dame Press, 1999), 68.

31. Blenkinsopp, "Miracles," 60.

32. Johnson, *Miracles*, 118.

33. Johnson, *Miracles*, 61.

34. Lindars, "Elijah, Elisha and Gospel Miracles," 74; Blenkinsopp, "Miracles," 63.

35. Walsh and Begg, "1–2 Kings," 176.

36. Lindars, "Elijah, Elisha and Gospel Miracles," 74–75.

37. Lindars, "Elijah, Elisha and Gospel Miracles," 64.

38. Johnson, *Miracles*, 118.

39. Collins, *Introduction to Hebrew Bible*, 559–60.

40. Collins, *Introduction to Hebrew Bible*, 570.

41. Collins, *Introduction to Hebrew Bible*, 573.

42. Collins, *Introduction to Hebrew Bible*, 66. See also Carmel McCarthy and William Riley, *The Old Testament Short Story* (Wilmington, DE: Michael Glazier, 1986), 140–41.

43. John P. M. Sweet, "The Theory of Miracles in the Wisdom of Solomon," in Moule, *Miracles*, 118–19.

44. Sweet, "Theory of Miracles," 115.

45. See Addison G. Wright, "Wisdom," in Brown, Fitzmyer, and Murphy, *The New Jerome Biblical Commentary*, 522.

CHAPTER 3

1. Raymond E. Brown, *Responses to 101 Questions on the Bible* (London: Geoffrey Chapman, 1991), 66.

2. E. P. Sanders, *Jesus and Judaism* (Minneapolis: Fortress Press, 1985), 173.

3. Barnabas Lindars, "Elijah, Elisha and the Gospel Miracles," in *Miracles: Cambridge Studies in Their Philosophy and History*, ed. C. F. D. Moule (London: A. R. Mowbray, 1965), 79.

4. Luke Timothy Johnson, *Miracles: God's Presence and Power in Creation* (Louisville, KY: Westminster John Knox Press, 2018), 140.

5. Johnson, *Miracles*, 148–49.

6. John P. Meier, *A Marginal Jew*, vol. 2, *Mentor, Message, and Miracles* (New York: Doubleday, 1994), 536.

7. Lindars, "Elijah, Elisha and Gospel Miracles," 77–78.

8. See Géza Vermes, *Jesus the Jew* (Philadelphia: Fortress Press, 1973), 72.

9. m.Taan. 3:8, cited in Vermes, *Jesus the Jew*, 70.

10. Joseph Blenkinsopp, "Miracles: Elisha and Hanina ben Dosa," in *Miracles in Jewish and Christian Antiquity*, ed. John C. Cavadini (Notre Dame, IN: University of Notre Dame Press, 1999), 71–77.

11. Vermes, *Jesus the Jew*, 72.

12. Blenkinsopp, "Miracles," 78.

13. Vermes, *Jesus the Jew*, 78–79.

14. For details, one might consult Larry Hurtado, *Lord Jesus Christ: Devotion to Jesus in Earliest Christianity* (Grand Rapids, MI: Eerdmans, 2005).

15. Jose Pagola, *Jesus: An Historical Approximation* (Miami: Convivium Press, 2009), 397. The Pauline reference is from Galatians 2:20.

16. Meier, *Marginal Jew*, 538.

17. Meier, *Marginal Jew*, 546.

18. Meier, *Marginal Jew*, 548. Actually, Meier provides seven characteristics, but in my judgment they may be reduced without any loss of intelligibility to the six that are outlined here. Johnson, *Miracles*, 167, humorously writes about John Meier: "I will not enter into discussion with the extraordinary volume of scholarly writing devoted to the miracles of Jesus as a historical figure...and will only note that exhaustive notes and bibliography for every aspect of every miracle account are provided by J. P. Meier. Readers who want to lose themselves in this labyrinth can begin with his notes."

19. Lindars, "Elijah, Elisha and Gospel Miracles," 78.

20. Lindars, "Elijah, Elisha and Gospel Miracles," 77.

21. In the apocryphal Gospels one finds examples of miracles that really are nothing more than a demonstration of the power of Jesus, and in that respect they are not of primary theological significance.

22. Alan Richardson, *An Introduction to the Theology of the New Testament* (New York: Harper & Row, 1958), 95.

23. Johnson, *Miracles*, 202–3.

24. Johnson, *Miracles*, 171.

25. Hubert J. Richards, *Philosophy of Religion*, 2nd ed. (Oxford: Heinemann, 2000), 85.

26. Richards, *Philosophy of Religion*, 86.

27. See Hugo A. Meynell, *God and the World* (London: SPCK, 1971), 89.

28. Meynell, *God and the World*, 90–93.

29. Richards, *Philosophy of Religion*, 87.

30. Hugh Montefiore, *The Miracles of Jesus* (London: SPCK, 2005).

31. Montefiore, *Miracles of Jesus*, 14.

32. Montefiore, *Miracles of Jesus*, 19.

33. Montefiore, *Miracles of Jesus*, 36.

34. Montefiore, *Miracles of Jesus*, 40.

35. Montefiore, *Miracles of Jesus*, 116.

36. Jeffrey John, *The Meaning in the Miracles* (Grand Rapids, MI: Eerdmans, 2001).

37. See note 6 above.

38. John, *Meaning in Miracles*, 22.

39. John, *Meaning in Miracles*, 14.

40. John, *Meaning in Miracles*, 13.

41. John, *Meaning in Miracles*, 15–16.

42. John, *Meaning in Miracles*, 24.

CHAPTER 4

1. Hubert J. Richards, *Philosophy of Religion*, 2nd ed. (Oxford: Heinemann, 2000), 85.

2. Alan Richardson, *An Introduction to the Theology of the New Testament* (New York: Harper & Row, 1958), 101.

3. Jeffrey John, *The Meaning in the Miracles* (Grand Rapids: Eerdmans, 2001), 68.

4. David Brown, *Tradition and Interpretation* (Oxford: Oxford University Press, 1999), 284.

5. Luke Timothy Johnson, *Miracles: God's Presence and Power in Creation* (Louisville, KY: Westminster John Knox Press, 2018), 208. A similar point of view, although from a contrasting ecclesial perspective, may be found in the summary article of Barry L. Blackburn, "The Miracles of Jesus," in *The Cambridge Companion to Miracles*, ed. Graham Twelftree (Cambridge: Cambridge University Press, 2011), 113–30.

6. Graham Stanton, "Message and Miracles," in *The Cambridge Companion to Jesus*, ed. Markus Bockmuehl (Cambridge: Cambridge University Press, 2001), 67.

7. John, *Meaning in Miracles*, 192.

8. John, *Meaning in Miracles*, 195.

9. John, *Meaning in Miracles*, 196.

10. John, *Meaning in Miracles*, 230.

11. John, *Meaning in Miracles*, 231.

12. Johnson, *Miracles*, 208.

13. Richardson, *Introduction to Theology of New Testament*, 100.

14. John, *Meaning in Miracles*, 73.

15. John, *Meaning in Miracles*, 74.

16. John, *Meaning in Miracles*, 76.

17. John, *Meaning in Miracles*, 77.

18. John, *Meaning in Miracles*, 76.

19. Brown, *Tradition*, 285.

20. John, *Meaning in Miracles*, 47.

21. Johnson, *Miracles*, 260–61.

22. John, *Meaning in Miracles*, 50.

23. John, *Meaning in Miracles*, 5.

24. John, *Meaning in Miracles*, 5.

25. John, *Meaning in Miracles*, 62–63.

26. John, *Meaning in Miracles*, 63–64.

27. Richardson, *Introduction to Theology of New Testament*, 102. Johnson, *Miracles*, 211, makes the same point: "This element of the feedings also points forward to Mark's account of the Last Supper, when, in a ritual act that anticipates and symbolizes his

ultimate act of obedience and service on the cross, [Jesus] shares bread and wine with his followers."

28. John, *Meaning in Miracles*, 216.

29. John, *Meaning in Miracles*, 218.

30. Raymond E. Brown, *The Gospel according to John*, vol. 1 (New York: Doubleday/Anchor Bible, 1966), 432.

31. John, *Meaning in Miracles*, 220.

CHAPTER 5

1. Benedicta Ward, "Monks and Miracle," in *Miracles in Jewish and Christian Antiquity*, ed. John C. Cavadini (Notre Dame, IN: University of Notre Dame Press, 1999), 128. See also Benedicta Ward, "Miracles in the Middle Ages," in *The Cambridge Companion to Miracles*, ed. Graham Twelftree (Cambridge: Cambridge University Press, 2011), 149–64.

2. Benedicta Ward, *Miracles and the Medieval Mind*, rev. ed. (Philadelphia: University of Pennsylvania Press, 1987), 1.

3. C. F. D. Moule, "The Vocabulary of Miracle," in *Miracles: Cambridge Studies in Their Philosophy and History*, ed. C. F. D. Moule (London: Mowbray, 1965), 235.

4. James Carleton Paget, "Miracles in Early Christianity," in *The Cambridge Companion to Miracles*, ed. Graham Twelftree (Cambridge: Cambridge University Press, 2011), 132.

5. G. W. H Lampe, "Miracles and Early Christian Apologetic," in *Miracles: Cambridge Studies in Their Philosophy and History*, ed. C. F. D. Moule (London: A. R. Mowbray, 1965), 206.

6. Eusebius, *Ecclesiastical History* 4.3.2.

7. Lampe, "Miracles and Early Christian Apologetic," 209.

8. Lampe, "Miracles and Early Christian Apologetic," 210.

9. Origen, *Contra Celsum* 1.28.

10. Lampe, "Miracles and Early Christian Apologetic," 211.

11. Tertullian, *Against Marcion* 4.36.13.

12. John A. McGuckin, *Westminster Handbook of Patristic Theology* (Louisville, KY: Westminster John Knox Press, 2004), 224.

13. Maurice Wiles, "Miracles in the Early Church," in Moule, *Miracles*, 224.

14. St. John Chrysostom, *Hom. in Matt.* 12.2; 14.3.

15. McGuckin, *Westminster Handbook of Patristic Theology*, 225.

16. Ward, "Monks and Miracle," 129.

17. Ward, "Monks and Miracle," 130–31.

18. Paget, "Miracles," 138.

19. Ward, "Miracles in the Middle Ages," 151.

20. Henry Chadwick, *Augustine of Hippo, A Life* (New York: Oxford University Press, 2009), 76–77.

21. Ward, "Monks and Miracle," 133.

22. The translation cited here is Augustine, *City of God*, trans. Henry Bettenson, ed. David Knowles (Harmondsworth: Penguin Books, 1972).

23. St. Augustine, *The Trinity*, intro., trans., and notes by Edmund Hill, OP, 2nd ed. (Hyde Park, NY: New City Press, 2012), 133–34.

24. Paul Ternant, "Miracle," in *Dictionary of Biblical Theology*, ed. Xavier Léon-Dufour, SJ (New York: Desclée, 1967), 317.

25. Ward, *Miracles and Medieval Mind*, 3.

26. Ward, *Miracles and Medieval Mind*, 3–4.

27. *De Utilitate Credendi* 16.34, cited in Ward, *Miracles and Medieval Mind*, 4.

28. *De Cura pro Mortuis Gerenda* 16.19, cited in Ward, *Miracles and Medieval Mind*, 4.

29. Louis Monden, *Signs and Wonders* (New York: Desclée, 1966), 42–43.

30. Monden, *Signs and Wonders*, 46.

31. Ward, *Miracles and Medieval Mind*, 214.

32. Anselm of Canterbury, *De Conceptu Virginali* 21.8, cited in Ward, *Miracles and Medieval Mind*, 4.

33. Ward, *Miracles and Medieval Mind*, 7.

34. Ward, "Miracles in the Middle Ages," 152.

35. Ralph Del Colle, "Miracles in Christianity," in Twelftree, *Cambridge Companion to Miracles*, 240.

36. Ward, "Miracles in the Middle Ages," 154.

37. Ward, "Miracles in the Middle Ages," 154.

38. Ward, "Miracles in the Middle Ages," 155.

39. Ward, "Miracles in the Middle Ages," 151.

40. Joseph Houston, *Reported Miracles* (Cambridge: Cambridge University Press, 1994), 21.

41. St. Thomas Aquinas, *Summa Contra Gentiles* 3.101.2–4.

42. Houston, *Reported Miracles,* 24.

43. St. Thomas Aquinas, *Summa Contra Gentiles* 3.99.9.

44. See *Summa Theologiae,* IIIa.43.4.

45. Surah 13.

46. Ward, *Miracles and Medieval Mind,* 15.

47. Related to eucharistic miracles but in an aside Louis Monden, *Signs and Wonders,* 61 writes, "Are there not some Baroque monstrances which display so tasteless a refinement of elaboration in symbolizing the inner richness of the Eucharistic mystery that they all but succeed in distracting our attention from its essence? The same may be said of miracles. They do attract attention, in some sense, by the fact that they are unusual, by the sense of surprise which is evoked by the unaccustomed; but excessive sensationalism would make them miss the mark. No doubt, a great effect will be produced to the extent that they satisfy man's thirst for the marvelous; but such an effect would inevitably be enmeshed in the passion of worldly curiosity, and, far from drawing attention to the real meaning of the miraculous occurrence, would force it into the background."

48. Ward, *Miracles and Medieval Mind,* 16–17.

49. Ward, *Miracles and Medieval Mind,* 214.

50. Ward, *Miracles and Medieval Mind,* 216.

51. Ward, "Monks and Miracle," 135–36. Ward's point of view may be found also, though with less historical detail, in Monden, *Signs and Wonders,* 36–57.

CHAPTER 6

1. Jane Shaw, *Miracles in Enlightenment England* (New Haven, CT: Yale University Press, 2006), 177.

2. Joseph Houston, *Reported Miracles: A Critique of Hume* (Cambridge: Cambridge University Press, 1994), 3.

3. Gerald R. Cragg, *The Church and the Age of Reason, 1648–1789* (Harmondsworth: Penguin Books, 1970), 13. See the useful summary of the controversies surrounding miracles in Jaroslav Pelikan, *Christian Doctrine and Modern Culture since 1700* (Chicago: University of Chicago Press, 1989), 62–66.

4. Shaw, *Miracles in Enlightenment*, 22.

5. Shaw, *Miracles in Enlightenment*, 25.

6. Shaw, *Miracles in Enlightenment*, 73.

7. Shaw, *Miracles in Enlightenment*, 73.

8. Shaw, *Miracles in Enlightenment*, 142–43.

9. R. M. Burns, *The Great Debate on Miracles from Joseph Glanville to David Hume* (Lewisburg: Bucknell University Press, 1981), 10, cited in Jane Shaw, *Miracles in Enlightenment*, 204.

10. Cited in Shaw, *Miracles in Enlightenment*, 178. See also Ralph Del Colle, "Miracles in Christianity," in *The Cambridge Companion to Miracles*, ed. Graham Twelftree (Cambridge: Cambridge University Press, 2011), 240–44.

11. John C. A. Gaskin, *Hume's Philosophy of Religion* (New York: Harper & Row, 1978), 125.

12. David Hume, "Of Miracles," in *Hume on Miracles*, ed. Stanley Weyman (Bristol: Thoemmes Press, 1996), 2. It is to this edition of the essay that direct reference for the most part is made.

13. David Hume, *An Enquiry Concerning Human Understanding*, ed. L. Selby-Bigge (Oxford: Oxford University Press, 1902), 109.

14. Hume, *An Enquiry*, 115–16.

15. Gaskin, *Hume's Philosophy*, 114.

16. Hume, "Of Miracles," 2.

17. Hume, *An Enquiry*, 126.

18. Gaskin, *Hume's Philosophy*, 115.

19. Del Colle, "Miracles in Christianity," 248.

20. Friedrich Schleiermacher, *On Religion: Speeches to Its Cultured Despisers* (New York: Harper and Row, 1958), 88.

21. Del Colle, "Miracles in Christianity," 249.

CHAPTER 7

1. Richard P. McBrien, *Catholicism*, 3rd ed. (New York: HarperCollins, 1994), 339.

2. Brian Hebblethwaite, *In Defense of Christianity* (New York: Oxford University Press, 2005), 105.

3. This phrase is taken from John P. Meier, *A Marginal Jew*, vol. 2, *Mentor, Message, and Miracles* (New York: Doubleday, 1994), 520.

4. Meier, *Marginal Jew*, 520–21.

5. Gerard Manley Hopkins, "God's Grandeur," in *Poems and Prose of Gerard Manley Hopkins*, selected with an introduction and notes by W. H. Gardner (New York: Penguin Books, 1985), 27.

6. McBrien, *Catholicism*, 340–41.

7. *The Church's Confession of Faith: A Catholic Catechism for Adults* (San Francisco: Ignatius Press, 1987), 130.

8. McBrien, *Catholicism*, 342.

9. Terence L. Nichols, *The Sacred Cosmos* (Grand Rapids: Brazos Press, 2003), 197.

10. Nichols, *Sacred Cosmos*, 184.

11. Nichols, *Sacred Cosmos*, 184.

12. Nichols, *Sacred Cosmos*, 184.

13. Nichols, *Sacred Cosmos*, 184–85.

14. Nichols, *Sacred Cosmos*, 188.

15. Nichols, *Sacred Cosmos*, 189.

16. Nichols, *Sacred Cosmos*, 189.

17. Nichols, *Sacred Cosmos*, 190.

18. Nichols, *Sacred Cosmos*, 191.

19. Nichols, *Sacred Cosmos*, 191.

20. Nichols, *Sacred Cosmos*, 193.

21. Nichols, *Sacred Cosmos*, 193.

22. Nichols, *Sacred Cosmos*, 195.

23. Nichols, *Sacred Cosmos*, 195, slightly adapted.

24. Rowan D. Williams, *Tokens of Trust: An Introduction to Christian Belief* (Louisville, KY: Westminster John Knox Press, 2007).

25. Williams, *Tokens of Trust*, 43–44.

26. Williams, *Tokens of Trust*, 44.

27. Williams, *Tokens of Trust*, 44–45.

28. Williams, *Tokens of Trust*, 48–49.

29. Williams, *Tokens of Trust*, 48.

30. John F. Haught, *The New Cosmic Story: Inside Our Awakening Universe* (New Haven, CT: Yale University Press, 2017).

31. Haught, *New Cosmic Story*, 191.

32. Haught, *New Cosmic Story*, 7.

33. Hebblethwaite, *Defense of Christianity*, 97–98, referencing E. P. Sanders, *The Historical Figure of Jesus* (London: Allen Lane, Penguin, 1993).

34. Hebblethwaite, *Defense of Christianity*, 98, citing Sanders, *The Historical Figure of Jesus*, 280.

35. Hebblethwaite, *Defense of Christianity*, 98

36. Hebblethwaite, *Defense of Christianity*, 105–6.

37. Austin Farrer, *Saving Belief* (London: Hodder and Stoughton, 1964), 83.

38. Hebblethwaite, *Defense of Christianity*, 106.

39. Hebblethwaite, *Defense of Christianity*, 107–8.

40. Hans Küng, *The Beginning of All Things: Science and Religion* (Grand Rapids: Eerdmans, 2007), 151.

41. Küng, *Beginning of All Things*, 151–52.

42. Küng, *Beginning of All Things*, 152.

43. Küng, *Beginning of All Things*, 153.

44. Küng, *Beginning of All Things*, 153–54.

45. Küng, *Beginning of All Things*, 155.

46. Küng, *Beginning of All Things*, 156.

47. Küng, *Beginning of All Things*, 156.

48. Küng, *Beginning of All Things*, 157.

49. Küng, *Beginning of All Things*, 157–58.

50. Küng, *Beginning of All Things*, 158.

51. Thomas Jay Oord, *The Nature of Love* (Atlanta: Chalice Press, 2010), 153.

52. Oord, *Nature of Love*, 153–54.

53. Oord, *Nature of Love*, 153–54.

54. Oord, *Nature of Love*, 147.

55. Oord, *Nature of Love*, 147–48.

56. Oord, *Nature of Love*, 148.
57. Oord, *Nature of Love*, 148.
58. Oord, *Nature of Love*, 148.
59. Oord, *Nature of Love*, 148.
60. Oord, *Nature of Love*, 148.
61. Oord, *Nature of Love*, 148.
62. Oord, *Nature of Love*, 149.
63. Oord, *Nature of Love*, 149.
64. Oord, *Nature of Love*, 149.
65. Oord, *Nature of Love*, 149–50.
66. Thomas E. Hosinski, *The Image of the Unseen God* (Maryknoll, NY: Orbis Books, 2017), 138.
67. Hosinski, *Image of Unseen God*, 138.
68. Hosinski, *Image of Unseen God*, 138–39.
69. Hosinski, *Image of Unseen God*, 139.
70. Hosinski, *Image of Unseen God*, 139.
71. Hosinski, *Image of Unseen God*, 140.
72. Gabriel Daly, *Asking the Father* (Dublin: Dominican Publications, 1982), 47–65.
73. Daly, *Asking the Father*, 48.
74. Daly, *Asking the Father*, 52.
75. Daly, *Asking the Father*, 55.
76. Daly, *Asking the Father*, 56.
77. Daly, *Asking the Father*, 56–57.
78. Daly, *Asking the Father*, 57.
79. Daly, *Asking the Father*, 59.
80. Luke Timothy Johnson, *Miracles: God's Presence and Power in Creation* (Louisville, KY: Westminster John Knox Press, 2018), 300. A similar point of view may be found throughout Louis Monden's, *Signs and Wonders* (New York: Desclée, 1966), e.g., 26–27: "It is clear that a miracle is to be envisioned as a direct prolongation of the Incarnation, as a perceptible showing forth of God's redemptive love….In this process by which God schools us—by a pedagogy which baffles description because it so lends itself to our human weakness—the miracle is yet a further step: it extends to its uttermost limit the divine condescension of the Incarnation."
81. Monden, *Signs and Wonders*, xi.

82. Monden, *Signs and Wonders*, 11.
83. Monden, *Signs and Wonders*, 26.
84. Monden, *Signs and Wonders*, 37.
85. Monden, *Signs and Wonders*, 56.
86. Monden, *Signs and Wonders*, 62.
87. For general background, see Owen F. Cummings, *John Macquarrie: A Master of Theology* (New York: Paulist Press, 2002).
88. All references will be to John Macquarrie, *Principles of Christian Theology*, rev. ed. (New York: Scribner's, 1977), esp. 247–53.
89. Macquarrie, *Principles of Christian Theology*, 247.
90. Macquarrie, *Principles of Christian Theology*, 247.
91. For details of an alternative approach to Macquarrie's, including a critique of Macquarrie, see Joseph Houston, *Reported Miracles* (Cambridge: Cambridge University Press, 1994), 83–102.
92. Macquarrie, *Principles of Christian Theology*, 249.
93. Macquarrie, *Principles of Christian Theology*, 249.
94. Macquarrie, *Principles of Christian Theology*, 250.
95. Macquarrie, *Principles of Christian Theology*, 250.
96. Macquarrie, *Principles of Christian Theology*, 252.
97. Macquarrie, *Principles of Christian Theology*, 252.
98. Macquarrie, *Principles of Christian Theology*, 253.
99. Macquarrie, *Principles of Christian Theology*, 253.
100. Macquarrie, *Principles of Christian Theology*, 253.

CHAPTER 8

1. Tina Beattie, *The Good Priest* (Leicester, UK: Troubadour Publishing, 2019), 19–21.
2. Reginald H. Fuller, *Interpreting the Miracles* (London: SCM Press, 1963), 123.
3. Gabriel Daly, *The Church: Always in Need of Reform* (Dublin: Dominican Publications, 2015), 119.

BIBLIOGRAPHY

Augustine. *City of God*. Translated by Henry Bettenson. Edited by David Knowles. Harmondsworth: Penguin Books, 1972.

———. *The Trinity*. Introduction, translation, and notes by Edmund Hill, OP. 2nd ed. Hyde Park, NY: New City Press, 2012.

Basinger, David. "What Is a Miracle?" In *The Cambridge Companion to Miracles*, edited by Graham W. Twelftree, 19–35. Cambridge: Cambridge University Press, 2011.

Bauckham, Richard. *Jesus and the Eyewitnesses*. Grand Rapids: Eerdmans, 2006.

Beattie, Tina. *The Good Priest*. Leicester, UK: Troubadour Publishing, 2019.

Blackburn, Barry L. "The Miracles of Jesus." In *The Cambridge Companion to Miracles*, edited by Graham H. Twelftree, 113–30. Cambridge: Cambridge University Press, 2011.

Blenkinsopp, Joseph. "Miracles: Elisha and Hanina ben Dosa." In *Miracles in Jewish and Christian Antiquity*, edited by John C. Cavadini, 57–81. Notre Dame, IN: University of Notre Dame Press, 1999.

Brown, David. *Tradition and Interpretation*. Oxford: Oxford University Press, 1999.

Brown, Raymond E. *Responses to 101 Questions on the Bible*. London: Geoffrey Chapman, 1991.

Catholic Church Deutsche Bischofskonferenz. *The Church's Confession of Faith*. Edited by Mark D. Jordan and Walter Kasper. San Francisco: Ignatius Press, 1987.

Cavadini, John C., ed. *Miracles in Jewish and Christian Antiquity*. Notre Dame, IN: University of Notre Dame Press, 1999.

Chadwick, Henry. *Augustine of Hippo: A Life*. Oxford: Oxford University Press, 2009.

Collins, John J. *Introduction to the Hebrew Bible*. 2nd ed. Minneapolis: Fortress Press, 2014.

Coogan, Michael D. "Joshua." In *The New Jerome Biblical Commentary*, edited by R. E. Brown, J. A. Fitzmyer, and R. E. Murphy, 110–31. Englewood Cliffs, NJ: Prentice-Hall, 1990.

Cottingham, John. *Why Believe?* New York: Continuum, 2009.

Coventry, John. *Christian Truth*. New York: Paulist Press, 1975.

Cragg, Gerald R. *The Church and the Age of Reason, 1648–1789*. Harmondsworth: Penguin Books, 1970.

Daly, Gabriel. *Asking the Father*. Dublin: Dominican Publications, 1979.

Gaskin, John C. A. *Hume's Philosophy of Religion*. New York: Harper and Row, 1978.

———. *The Quest for Eternity: An Outline of the Philosophy of Religion*. Harmondsworth: Penguin Books, 1984.

Haught, John F. *The New Cosmic Story: Inside Our Awakening Universe*. New Haven, CT: Yale University Press, 2017.

Hebblethwaite, Brian. *In Defense of Christianity*. New York: Oxford University Press, 2005.

Hefling, Charles. "Miracle." In *The New Dictionary of Theology*, edited by Joseph A. Komonchak, Mary Collins, and Dermot A. Lane, 661–64. Collegeville, MN: Liturgical Press/Michael Glazier, 1987.

Houston, Joseph. *Reported Miracles: A Critique of Hume*. Cambridge: Cambridge University Press, 1994.

Hume, David. *Enquiry Concerning Human Understanding* (1748), various modern publishers.

Humphreys, Colin. *The Miracles of Exodus: A Scientist's Discovery of the Extraordinary Natural Causes of the Biblical Stories*. New York: Continuum, 2003.

John, Jeffrey. *The Meaning in the Miracles*. Grand Rapids: Eerdmans, 2001.

Johnson, Luke Timothy. *Miracles: God's Presence and Power in Creation*. Louisville, KY: Westminster John Knox Press, 2018.

Küng, Hans. *The Beginning of All Things: Science and Religion*. Grand Rapids: Eerdmans, 2007.

Lampe, Geoffrey. "Miracles and Early Christian Apologetic." In *Miracles: Cambridge Studies in Their Philosophy and History*, edited by C. F. D. Moule, 203–18. London: Mowbray, 1965.

Lienhard, Joseph T. *The Bible, the Church, and Authority*. Collegeville, MN: Liturgical Press, 1995.

Lindars, Barnabas. "Elijah, Elisha and the Gospel Miracles." In *Miracles: Cambridge Studies in Their Philosophy and History*, edited by C. F. D. Moule, 61–79. London: A. R. Mowbray, 1965.

———. "Miracle." In *A New Dictionary of Christian Theology*, edited by Alan Richardson and John S. Bowden, 370–72. London: SCM Press, 1983.

McBrien, Richard P. *Catholicism*. 3rd ed. New York: HarperCollins, 1994.

McCarthy, Carmel, and William Riley. *The Old Testament Short Story*. Wilmington, DE: Michael Glazier, 1986.

McKenzie, John L. *Dictionary of the Bible*. Milwaukee: Bruce, 1965.

Meier, John P. *A Marginal Jew*. Vol. 2: *Mentor, Message and Miracles*. New York: Doubleday, 1994.

Meynell, Hugo A. *God and the World*. London: SPCK, 1971.

Moberly, Walter L. "Miracles in the Hebrew Bible." In *The Cambridge Companion to Miracles*, edited by Graham H. Twelftree, 57–74. Cambridge: Cambridge University Press, 2011.

Monden, Louis. *Signs and Wonders: A Study of the Miraculous Element in Religion*. New York: Desclée, 1966.

Montefiore, Hugh. *The Miracles of Jesus*. London: SPCK, 2005.

Moule, C. F. D., ed. *Miracles: Cambridge Studies in Their Philosophy and History*. London: Mowbray, 1965.

———. "The Vocabulary of Miracle." In *Miracles: Cambridge Studies in Their Philosophy and History*, edited by C. F. D. Moule, 235–38. London: Mowbray, 1965.

Mullin, Robert B. "Miracle." In *The Oxford Companion to Christian Thought*, edited by Adrian Hastings et al., 438–40. Oxford: Oxford University Press, 2000.

Novakovic, Lidija. "Miracles in Second Temple and Early Rabbinic Judaism." In *The Cambridge Companion to Miracles*, edited by Graham Twelftree, 95–112. Cambridge: Cambridge University Press, 2011.

O'Malley, John W. *Four Cultures of the West*. Cambridge: The Belknap Press of Harvard University, 2004.

Oord, Thomas Jay. *The Nature of Love: A Theology*. St. Louis, MO: Chalice Press, 2010.

Paget, James Carleton. "Miracles in Early Christianity." In *The Cambridge Companion to Miracles*, edited by Graham Twelftree, 131–48. Cambridge: Cambridge University Press, 2011.

Pelikan, Jaroslav. *Christian Doctrine and Modern Culture since 1700*. Chicago: University of Chicago Press, 1989.

Richards, Hubert J. *The Miracles of Jesus*. Mystic, CT: Twenty-Third Publications, 1986.

———. *Philosophy of Religion*. 2nd ed. Oxford: Heinemann, 2000.

Richardson, Alan. *An Introduction to the Theology of the New Testament*. New York: Harper and Row, 1958.

Ross, John P. "Some Notes on Miracle in the Old Testament." In *Miracles: Cambridge Studies in Their Philosophy and History*, edited by C. F. D. Moule, 43–60. New York: Mowbray, 1965.

Senior, Donald. "The Bones of Jesus: Bodily Resurrection and Christian Faith." *Origins* 37 (2008): 642–47.

Shaw, Jane. *Miracles in Enlightenment England*. New Haven, CT: Yale University Press, 2006.

Smart, Ninian. *Philosophers and Religious Truth*. London: SCM Press, 1964.

Stanton, Graham. *The Gospels and Jesus*. 2nd ed. New York: Oxford University Press, 2002.

———. "Message and Miracles." In *The Cambridge Companion to Jesus*, edited by Markus Bockmuehl, 67. Cambridge: Cambridge University Press, 2001.

Sweet, John P. M. "The Theory of Miracles in the Wisdom of Solomon." In *Miracles: Cambridge Studies in Their Philosophy and History*, edited by C. F. D. Moule, 113–26. London: Mowbray, 1965.

Swinburne, Richard. *The Concept of Miracle*. London: Macmillan, 1970.

Ternant, Paul. "Miracle." In *Dictionary of Biblical Theology*, edited by Xavier Léon-Dufour, SJ, 317–22. New York: Desclée, 1967.

Twelftree, Graham H., ed. *The Cambridge Companion to Miracles*. Cambridge: Cambridge University Press, 2011.

Ullrich, Lothar. "Miracle." In *Handbook of Catholic Theology*, edited by Wolfgang Beinert and Francis Schüssler Fiorenza, 481–84. New York: Crossroad, 2000.

Vermes, Geza. *Jesus the Jew*. Philadelphia: Fortress Press, 1973.

Walsh, Jerome T., and Christopher T. Begg. "1–2 Kings." In *The New Jerome Biblical Commentary*, edited by R. E. Brown, J. A. Fitzmyer, and R. E. Murphy, 160–85. Englewood Cliffs, NJ: Prentice Hall, 1990.

Ward, Benedicta. *Miracles and the Medieval Mind*. Rev. ed. Philadelphia: University of Pennsylvania Press, 1987.

———. "Miracles in the Middle Ages." In *The Cambridge Companion to Miracles*, edited by Graham Twelftree, 149–64. Cambridge: Cambridge University Press, 2011.

———. "Monks and Miracle." In *Miracles in Jewish and Christian Antiquity*, edited by John C. Cavadini, 127–37. Notre Dame, IN: University of Notre Dame Press, 1999.

Wiles, Maurice F. "Miracles in the Early Church." In *Miracles: Cambridge Studies in Their Philosophy and History*, edited by C. F. D. Moule, 219–34. London: Mowbray, 1965.

———. *Reason to Believe*. Harrisburg, PA: Trinity Press International, 1999.

Williams, Rowan D. *Tokens of Trust: An Introduction to Christian Belief*. Louisville, KY: Westminster John Knox Press, 2007.

Woodward, Kenneth. *Making Saints*. New York: Simon & Schuster, 1990.

Wright, Addison G. "Wisdom." In *The New Jerome Biblical Commentary*, edited by R. E. Brown, J. A. Fitzmyer, and R. E. Murphy, 510–22. Englewood Cliffs, NJ: Prentice Hall, 1990.

Wright, N. T. "God's Way of Acting." *The Christian Century* 115, no. 35 (December 16, 1998): 1215–17.

Zachman, Randall C. "The Meaning of Biblical Miracles in Light of the Modern Quest for Truth." In *Miracles in Jewish and Christian Antiquity*, edited by John C. Cavadini, 1–18. Notre Dame, IN: University of Notre Dame Press, 1999.